NO BENEFIT

NO BENEFIT

Crisis in America's Health Insurance Industry

Lawrence D. Weiss

Westview Press
BOULDER • SAN FRANCISCO • OXFORD

Published in 1992 in the United States of America by Westview Press, Inc., 5500 Central Avenue, Boulder, Colorado 80301-2877, and in the United Kingdom by Westview Press, 36 Lonsdale Road, Summertown, Oxford OX2 7EW

Library of Congress Cataloging-in-Publication Data
Weiss, Lawrence David.
No benefit : crisis in America's health insurance industry / Lawrence D. Weiss.
p. cm.
Includes bibliographical references and index.
ISBN 0-8133-1215-9
1. Insurance, Health—United States. 2. Medical care, Cost of—United States. I. Title.
[DNLM: 1. Delivery of Health Care—economics—United States. 2. Health Policy—economics—United States. 3. Insurance, Health—economics—United States. W 275 AA1 W42n]
HG9396.W45 1992
368.3'82'00973—dc20
DNLM/DLC
for Library of Congress

92-18113
CIP

Printed and bound in the United States of America

The paper used in this publication meets the requirements of the American National Standard for Permanence of Paper for Printed Library Materials Z39.48-1984.

10 9 8 7 6 5 4 3 2 1

To all those who have suffered or
died as victims of a health care system dedicated to
maximum profit rather than universal access

contents

preface

How I came to write this book is something of an irony. One day just four or five years ago I was reading the *Anchorage Daily News,* my hometown newspaper, and I happened upon a short article in the business section. The gist of the article was that in the previous year the cost of health care services and commodities had risen by some percentage—about 9 or 10 percent. A few weeks later I ran across another brief article in the business section of the *News.* This article noted that in the same year, health insurance premiums had increased by a much larger percentage, perhaps 20 or 30 percent (I don't recall now). In any case this struck me as very odd indeed. A quick check in the *United States Statistical Abstract* and one or two other sources verified that this appeared to be a common pattern over time.

If the cost of health insurance premiums is pegged to the cost of health care services and commodities, I thought, why had the cost of health insurance premiums escalated at a rate two or three times higher than the cost of health care itself? And if the cost of health insurance is not bound closely to the cost of health care, then what does determine the cost of health insurance? That simple quandary nagged at me with unrelenting persistence because of the social importance of the dramatically rising cost of health insurance premiums. The consequences of this have wreaked havoc with the lives of millions of families across the United States. The slashing of health benefits has been a major cause of strike activity for several years. Unpaid medical bills have become the most common cause of recent personal bankruptcies. Tens of millions of residents have little or no access to health care in the United States, and their numbers increase alarmingly every year. This is a fundamental national social problem with dire consequences for the American people.

With some hesitation I tentatively began to probe the baffling and esoteric world of private health insurance. Perhaps the first surprise I encountered early in my research was that there was no book-length critical analysis of the health insurance industry. There were books about life insurance or insurance in general, insurance textbooks, and life/ health insurance statistical reference books, but no critical book-length analysis of the health insurance industry. This lack of readily available information forced me to dig deeper than I had originally intended. After all, I started out to answer what I initially thought was a straightforward question. The irony is that to this day I have not adequately answered the original question I posed to myself, although I now believe annual variations in the cost of health insurance premiums are tied more closely to industry investment strategies rather than to variations in the cost of health care. Nevertheless, as my research progressed I came to realize that the issue of health insurance was far more encompassing and far more significant than I ever imagined. I had begun to piece together an enormous tapestry—an industry with threads entwining the lives of every resident in the United States. I began to understand this emerging creation as a portrayal of the social consequences of private health insurance. As the panorama of wasteful, brutal, and inhumane social consequences grew and unfolded before me, it became clear that this was indeed an industry with no benefit. I felt it was important to share these findings with everyone struggling to create a national health care system equally accessible to all.

Finally, I would like to acknowledge just a few of the people who supported me during the stressful and lengthy process of theoretical formulation, research, and writing that ultimately resulted in this book. Dr. Frank Goldsmith encouraged my research and sent me volumes of data. Dr. Tom Bodenhiemer's brilliant work in this field inspired me. The late Ben Riskin documented in writing during his last weeks of life important information about the historic role of labor in the struggle for national health care. Dr. John Booker remained a close friend and colleague despite my inability for a couple of years to discuss anything except the health insurance industry. Dean Wayne Miller and Chairperson Jack Peterson supported faculty research and helped me find the resources to do it. Carlette Ivory gave timely and cheerful clerical support. The staff at the Health Sciences and Consortium Libraries at the University of Alaska–Anchorage were very helpful. Dean Birkenkamp and Jim Fieser at Westview Press recognized the value of this work and supported me fully throughout the process. Lastly, I thank my dear wife, Christy Smith, who listened politely and did not seek a divorce despite innumerable one-sided dinnertime discussions about the health insurance industry.

Lawrence D. Weiss

chapter one

Placing the Social Fact of Private Health Insurance in Perspective

In the United States having or not having adequate private health insurance has become synonymous with having or not having adequate access to health care. The health insurance industry has been desperately seeking to keep the association between private insurance and access inseparable in the public's mind. It is, however, a spurious and demonstrably harmful association. The Organization for Economic Cooperation and Development (OECD) is composed of twenty-two countries, including most of Europe, Japan, Canada, the United States, New Zealand, and Australia. Most of these countries have virtually no commercial private health insurance industry. Data from 1986 indicate that compared with these industrialized nations of the world the United States ranked first in average per capita spending on health care. According to George J. Schieber, director of the Office of Research, Health Care Financing Administration: "Spending in the United States was 38 percent higher than Canada, the second highest country; 49 percent higher than Sweden, the third highest country; 184 percent higher than the United Kingdom, the 17th ranked country; and 600 percent higher than Greece, the last ranked country" (U.S. Congress 1989e, 24).

Although the United States spends the most on health care, life expectancy in the United States ranks eighth among the OECD countries and infant mortality ranks twentieth.

Probing into perceived differences among national health care systems, *Health Management Quarterly* and the Harvard School of Public Health teamed up with Louis Harris and Associates in late 1988 to simultaneously survey populations in the United States, Canada, and Great Britain about attitudes toward various health care systems (Blendon 1989). Great Britain has a national health service characterized by a public-sector health care delivery system funded by the government. Canada has a national health insurance system with a private-sector health care delivery system financed with public funds. Private health insurance plays no significant role in either of these two countries. Finally, the United States has a private-sector health care delivery system funded predominantly from private sources.

Life expectancy in Canada is significantly higher than in the United States and Great Britain, where it is about the same. Infant mortality is highest in the United States, followed by Great Britain and then Canada. There are especially striking differences in the average per capita cost of these systems, as noted previously. Another measure of cost is health care spending as a percentage of gross national product (GNP). In 1986 this spending was 11.1 percent in the United States, 8.5 percent in Canada, and 6.2 percent in Great Britain (Blendon 1989). The unusually low percentage in Great Britain is the result of the deliberate attempt for more than a decade by the conservative government to starve the national health service and privatize it as much as possible. In light of this history the rather positive survey responses of the British are especially remarkable. The survey responses were as follows:.

- Thirteen percent of the Americans responded that there was a time in the past twelve months when they could not get medical care they needed. Only 4 percent of the Canadians and 5 percent of the British so responded.
- Of these respondents, 58 percent of the Americans indicated that the main reasons they did not get medical help was because of lack of money or insurance. Among Canadians 14 percent responded similarly, as did a mere 2 percent among the British respondents.
- Fully 89 percent of Americans viewed the U.S. health care system as requiring fundamental change. The comparable figures for respondents evaluating their own health care systems are 43 percent for Canada and 69 percent for Great Britain.
- Ninety-five percent of the Canadians and 80 percent of the British polled preferred their own health care systems to the one in the United States.
- Twenty-nine percent of the Americans surveyed preferred the British health care system to their own, and 61 percent preferred the Canadian health care system to their own.

No Human Right

There is no human right to health care in the United States. It is a commodity to be bought and sold when there is an effective market and to be ignored when there is not. The unique hegemony in the United States of marketable health care commodities has led to a series of social contradictions in our society—and ultimately to social crisis.

Every physician/entrepreneur who arbitrarily raises prices or performs needless medical procedures to maximize income contributes to the rising cost of health care (Physicians Who Profit from Tests 1990). The social price paid for the unlimited pursuit of personal gain is overtreated patients (who have cash or adequate insurance) and undertreated victims (who lack sufficient cash or insurance).

Each hospital that builds a new wing on speculation or buys trendy high-tech equipment to create another "profit center" passes on these excessive costs to everyone paying hospital bills. This strategy maximizes income for the hospital yet puts hospital care further out of reach for people with insufficient cash or insurance.

Every health insurer who denies applicants, charges higher rates, or attaches special exclusions on policies as the result of medical examinations does so to minimize payment of benefits and increase profits. The social consequence of this is the escalating production of uninsured, underinsured, and uninsurable people across the nation.

Entrepreneurs and corporations in these private sectors of health care act to maximize their profit. The social consequence of their individual actions is a vast, growing army of uninsured or underinsured people who are blocked access to health care. Infant mortality and life expectancy rates in the United States continue to fall further behind the rest of the industrialized world. Thus, the central social question is: Should health care in the United States be a commodity or a right? In every other industrialized OECD nation, the predominant concept is health care as a right. In the United States, it is health care as a commodity, which is the principal reason health care costs skyrocket while statistically the health of Americans falls further and further behind.

Special Interests, Profit, and the State

During the twentieth century the development of the U.S. health care system was largely a history of physicians, hospitals, and insurance companies jockeying their respective positions to maximize profits while accommodating needs of the other players. The role of the state, that is, the public sector, has been to help private-sector players increase their income through favorable legislation while simultaneously providing some care for the country's residents who were pushed out of the private sector because they had ceased to be part of the "effective market." In this way the state also helped to blunt political opposition to a health care system based on the financial needs of the major players rather than the health needs of the public.

The private health insurance industry is the keystone of the bizarre and dysfunctional health care edifice now burdening the American people. The industry's structure and conflicting interests prevent it from effectively controlling physician and hospital costs or quality of care. The industry's overriding goal of profit rather than universal service is the single greatest obstacle to health care access. At the same time, the industry's political clout enables it to protect its interests and block effective reforms.

The insurance industry is one of the wealthiest industries in the economy. It translates that wealth into massive political influence to protect its interests, which are inextricably tied to the health care system status quo. The health insurance industry contributes directly to excessive costs of health care because its profits are determined in large part by investing revenue from premiums. The higher the premiums, the greater the potential investment profits. The insurance industry has little interest in low health care costs because they would directly affect its bottom line. The industry profits from exorbitant malpractice insurance premiums while ignoring the system of "self-regulation" that allows dangerous physicians to practice. The industry has historically encouraged the escalation of hospital and physician charges and now does little to effectively curtail them. The insurance industry has enjoyed legalized cartel status to pursue profits to the detriment of alternative forms of health care organization. Corruption, fraud, greed, and mismanagement are widespread in the industry and have disastrous consequences for those who have relied on financially unsound companies for health insurance. Finally, people are aware of the role that private health insurers have played. The industry is neither liked nor supported by the public.

The health insurance industry is not the only organized interest responsible for a deeply flawed health care system, but it is the most influential. Elimination of private health insurance in the United States will not alone solve all the structural problems of health care, but eradication of the industry will clear away defective groundwork upon which the system is built. With continued struggle, the rest will follow. The private health insurance industry can be replaced with a national health care system that will provide high-quality preventive and acute health care to all residents of the United States as a right—and at no charge. The concept is not wild-eyed social experimentation. This kind of national health system has a long-proven history in most industrialized countries. In the United States the implementation of such a system is simply a political question.

The Argument's Journey

Chapter 2 lays down the historical and economic groundwork necessary for understanding the contemporary role of the insurance industry in general and the health insurance industry in particular. A brief analysis of the historical development of the structure of U.S. health care in the twentieth century is developed. It relies substantially on Paul Starr's brilliant *Social Transformation of American Medicine,* which is in part a history of entrepreneurial providers and private insurers who accommodated the financial aspirations and needs of each other while jointly fending off alternative health care systems that would have better served the needs of the American people. This chapter also recounts a history of massive influence peddling among federal and state governments that resulted in major concessions to professional organizations dominated by physicians, hospitals, and private insurers. These accommodations and concessions have determined the current structure of health care in the United States.

The commercial insurance industry has become one of the wealthiest industries in the United States. During the past few decades commercial insurers eroded the dominating market share of Blue Cross/Blue Shield ("the Blues"). However, in a dramatic transformation of the market in the past two decades, self-insured enterprises grabbed a huge portion of the health insurance market away from both the Blues and commercial insurers. There are indications that the number of commercial and even Blue Cross/Blue Shield insurers will decrease in the coming decade because of failures and mergers. Additional important trends in recent decades indicate that private health insurance has been insuring a falling proportion of all insured persons compared with the public sector and a falling proportion of the total population. Meanwhile, in both relative and absolute terms the number of uninsured has steadily increased.

Chapter 3 is a detailed discussion of who the uninsured are in the United States today and how they are produced by private health insurers. Some of those at high risk as uninsured include children and young adults, minorities, and single mothers. The usually uninsured number about 37 million, the periodically uninsured number more than 60 million, and the inadequately insured total about 60 million. Private health insurance is clearly a system that does not provide adequate access to health care for a very large proportion of people in the United States. The uninsured are increasingly generated by private insurers trying to maximize profit or minimize financial loss. The uninsured or inadequately insured are produced as a function of inferior benefits, expensive health insurance premiums, high deductibles, and costly coinsurance. Others are produced by long waiting periods, major illnesses, or medical underwriting, that is, the medical examination of individuals in order to determine if they are insurable and under what conditions.

Most health insurance in the United States is made available through the workplace. Chapter 4 focuses on the social consequences of employer strategies for coping with the rising cost of health insurance. Some of these strategies include shifting by various means more of the cost to employees and dependents, eliminating health care benefits for employees, dependents, or both, reducing or eliminating health insurance for retirees and dependents, and switching from commercial to often inferior self-insured plans. Other strategies involve the increasing use of managed care programs such as health maintenance organizations (HMOs) or preferred provider organizations (PPOs). The ultimate outcome of many of these strategies is increased production of uninsured or inadequately insured residents.

Fraud, corruption, and misrepresentation are widespread in the insurance industry, annually producing hundreds of thousands, perhaps millions, of victims. The sums of money involved in this industry are phenomenal, and regulatory safeguards are an ineffective patchwork. Chapter 5 discusses the elderly, who are routinely victimized by high-pressure, unethical insurance salespeople selling inferior medigap and long-term care policies. Greedy and fraudulent insurance corporation con artists sell worthless policies to thousands of victims, declare insolvency, then skip to another state to repeat the scam. Every year several current and former insurance commissioners and high-placed industry regulators are indicted for fraud, corruption, misapplication of funds, and other crimes. Major commercial insurers have bilked the government out of billions of dollars in Medicare funds, and additional huge sums of money are regularly involved in kickback schemes between insurance brokers and corporate benefits purchasers. Small businesses are routinely fleeced by insurance associations and trusts managed by fraudulent or incompetent operators.

Chapter 6 discusses the issues of insurance cartels, monopoly, monopsony, and related federal and state legislation. The messy concept of "free enterprise" has not been much of an obstacle to insurers. With the help of proindustry government policy, the insurance industry in general and in some respects the health insurance industry in particular have enjoyed the freedoms of conspiracy, price fixing, boycott of services (e.g., refusing to sell insurance in a state with stringent regulations), carving up territories, and standardizing product lines (i.e., selling similar policies in order to avoid competition on that basis). The result for people attempting to purchase health insurance has been fewer choices and higher prices. The halcyon days of cartel-like behavior may be somewhat curtailed, however, as public pressure for trust-busting emerges at both the federal and state levels.

By all accounts, the 1990s will be the decade of commercial insurance corporation insolvencies and mergers. Chapter 7 discusses the magnitude of the situation and probable effects on the American people. There are numerous documented similarities between the insurance industry now and the savings and loan industry on the eve of the catastrophe of the 1980s. Increased competition from banks and other financial institutions, excessive junk bond holdings, fraud and mismanagement, greed, and declining real estate portfolios are just a few of the reasons why the insurance industry is financially shaky. One-third of the largest insurance companies in the United States are expected to fail or merge in the coming decade. State guarantee funds, designed to protect people whose insurance companies fail, are entirely inadequate to deal with anticipated massive insolvencies of multiple major insurers. The end result of this process will be a concentration of market control in the hands of fewer corporations, increasing insurance prices, fewer policy choices, and more uninsured people with little or no access to health care.

The public sector is far more efficient than the private sector when it comes to providing health insurance to the American people. Chapter 8 discusses the fact that one-third or more of each dollar paid for commercial health insurance goes toward nonmedical expenses such as profit, advertising, dividends, swollen administrators' salaries and perks, and fancy office space. This amount is approximately ten times what it would cost the public sector to deliver the same health insurance. A welter of forms and bureaucratic red tape bloat administrative expenses in every hospital and every physician's office. The paperwork and bureaucracy alone discourage access to health care for many people. Insurance companies have little incentive to compete on the basis of price, and they have limited ability to reduce the cost of medical services. The result is that people pay greatly for private health insurance yet receive less health care than they would with public health insurance.

Chapter 9 reviews a selection of federal and state legislation nominally designed to address cost and access issues in health care. Special attention is paid to the role of private health insurance or its absence in each plan reviewed. Recommendations offered by a range of health professionals' associations and organized labor are analyzed. Proposals from the private sector by the insurance industry and other sectors of industry are also reviewed. In addition, the political power of insurance industry lobbyists to block meaningful health care reform is discussed.

Finally, Chapter 10 briefly summarizes the main ideas explicated in this study. The insurance industry in general is in a period of massive change and restructuring as a result of both internal and external contradictions. This restructuring will cause increased suffering and victimization of millions of residents who will lose their health insurance, money, access to health care, and finally, for many, their health. Yet many political forces advocate the elimination of private health insurance, and their power is substantial and increasing.

chapter two

Historical Development and Current Profile of the Commercial Health Insurance Industry

Whoever provides medical care or pays the costs of illness stands to gain the gratitude and good will of the sick and their families. The prospect of these good-will returns to investment in health care creates a powerful motive for governments and other institutions to intervene in the economics of medicine. . . . On more narrowly commercial grounds, insurance companies also gain advantage from serving as middlemen. To be the intermediary in the costs of sickness is a strategic role that confers social and political as well as strictly economic gains.

—*Paul Starr,* The Social Transformation of American Medicine

Historical Development

The dominant position of commercial health insurance is quite a recent phenomenon in the history of the United States. Nearly 200 years ago Congress established a compulsory hospital insurance plan for American merchant seamen. More than half a century later, a decade before the Civil War, a few commercial health insurance companies set up shop in America only to fail in bankruptcy a short time afterward. In 1877 the Granite Cutters established the first union-based sickness plan, which was established to help maintain an income during periods of sickness-related absences from work. High costs, however, kept such benefits from spreading rapidly. During the first couple of decades in the twentieth century only a very small proportion of the population was covered by sickness benefits through various benefit societies, fraternal orders, and union locals (Starr 1982, 240–242).

During the period 1912–1920 the American Association for Labor Legislation (AALL) conducted the first major campaign for a national health insurance plan. AALL, initially a group of academics and intellectuals, was joined by professional organizations of nurses, public health officers, and others. In 1912 Theodore Roosevelt included national health insurance as a major plank on the Bull Moose ticket during his presidential campaign. By 1920 public health insurance proposals had been introduced in sixteen states. Pushed by organized labor, women's organizations, and Governor Al Smith, such legislation passed in the New York State Senate (Riskin 1991).

A Prussian and a Bolshevik Plot

The American Medical Association (AMA) at first ignored the movement. Samuel Gompers, president of the American Federation of Labor (AFL), was against federal legislation for workers' benefits in general. He thought that such widely available benefits might undermine the ability of labor unions to attract workers because the unions were built upon their unique ability to negotiate such benefits. Leaders of industry were generally against compulsory health insurance because they did not want to pay for it. Finally, the commercial insurance industry was perhaps the most vehement opponent of national health insurance because the plan included funeral benefits. Top insurance companies such as Metropolitan Life and Prudential sold a couple hundred million dollars' worth of funeral insurance annually, and they had no intention of losing that business. The broad movement for national health insurance came under severe attack after the United States entered World War I in 1917. By then physicians had come out firmly against the idea, and government propagandists had labeled national health insurance a Prussian plot because of its similarity to the German social insurance system (Starr 1982, 242–254).

During the anti-Communist hysteria immediately after World War I national health insurance was conveniently relabeled a Bolshevik plot by those allied against it. This combination of social forces and effective (though inconsistent) ideology blocked the expected national health insurance proposals in all sixteen states and generally quashed progressives during the 1920s (Riskin 1991). With the depression of the 1930s the issue of national health insurance reemerged. Absent for political reasons was the funeral benefit. Among reformers the focus on health insurance was stronger because of the rising costs of medical care. Predictably, the AMA was united and adamantly opposed to the concept (Starr 1982, 254–270).

Blue Cross and the American Hospital Association

Another development during the early 1930s would shape the nature of the U.S. health care industry for decades to come. It began with the concerns of hospital administrators. They found that beginning in the late 1920s and continuing into the depression years their patient loads were falling off, unpaid patient bills were escalating, and consequently hospital income was declining. A number of hospitals during this period developed prepaid medical expenses programs to stabilize their incomes. These rapidly developed into plans barely differentiated from localized insurance plans for hospital expenses. Because insurance was regulated at the state level, several of these plans faced unwanted state pressure to formally reorganize as insurance companies. The American Hospital Association (AHA) and a number of local hospital associations had a better idea. Why not pursue nonprofit status, an exemption from state insurance regulations, and virtual regional monopolies?

> The special enabling legislation sought by the AHA conferred the following advantages and privileges on the proposed hospital service corporations: exemption from the general insurance laws of the state; status as a charitable and benevolent organization; exemption from the obligation of maintaining the reserves required of commercial insurers; and tax exemption. The major justification offered in support of the special enabling legislation was the promise of service to the community, and particularly to low income families. (Law 1976, 8)

In 1934 the first such legislation was adopted by the State of New York. A mere four years later thirty-eight Blue Cross plans had enrolled 1.4 million persons. During the same period of time commercial health insurance companies provided hospital insurance to fewer than one-tenth that number. By 1945 Blue Cross enabling legislation had been adopted in thirty-five states and local plans claimed about three-fifths of the hospital insurance market. Within a couple of decades such legislation had been adopted in just about every state. Thus were born the individual Blue Cross plans across the nation and the Blue Cross Association, a nationwide trade organization. Furthermore, the enabling legislation in most states was worded in such a manner that no other organization could be established with comparable state benefits to compete with the local Blue Cross plans: "The combination of public enabling legislation and the private power of the AHA has assured that there is only one Blue Cross organization in any given area and that it is, to some degree, controlled by the hospitals" (Law 1976, 11).

Republicans and Dixiecrats

Back in the late 1930s, however, serious differences of opinion began to surface among various agencies and departments within the Roosevelt government regarding national health insurance. In response to massive demonstrations across the nation in 1937, the original draft of the Social Security Act included health care coverage (Riskin 1991). During summer 1938 the more progressive government elements convened a national conference in Washington, D.C., to discuss their proposed national health program. In a renewed burst of progressive national activity, more than 150 reformers and representatives of farmers' organizations, labor, and the health professions came to this conference. But it was all for naught: The 1938 elections witnessed the emergence of a new crop of Republicans and Dixiecrats who sabotaged progressive social policy until World War II began. Then the nation had other pressing concerns (Starr 1982, 274–278). Despite a 1942 national poll indicating that three of every four Americans favored national health insurance, the coordinated political movement for national health insurance had been sapped (Riskin 1991).

The AMA Fights "Socialized Medicine"

In 1945 President Truman revived hopes for a national health insurance plan by announcing his support for a proposal similar to those made in the late 1930s. Public reaction was mixed. Those in higher income brackets detested it, and those with lower incomes supported it. As might be expected, the AMA was vehemently against the proposal and enlisted a massive, sophisticated public relations and lobbying campaign to see that it was thwarted. At that time it was the most expensive lobbying campaign ever conducted. "The AMA had as its allies those who ran community organizations, the media of opinion, the large corporations" (Starr 1982, 282). Once again the AMA and their allies stirred up the pot of vicious anticommunism to attack "socialized medicine," and the proposal withered. As attention turned to the Korean War, the proposal died.

Despite the phenomenal growth of Blue Cross plans throughout the nation in the first couple of decades of their existence, during the early 1950s private commercial hospital insurance grew at an even faster rate, eventually overtaking Blue Cross in market share. By 1951 Blue Cross had enrolled nationally about 37 million persons, whereas the commercial insurers had enrolled 40 million. Blue Cross was not able to compete successfully with the commercial health insurers during the balance of the 1950s and 1960s. By 1969 Blue Cross plans had enrolled 67 million civilians under age sixty-five, but that represented only 37 percent of the market. Nearly all the rest were insured by the commercial insurance companies (Law 1976, 11).

Blue Shield was established at about the same time as Blue Cross and was similarly initiated for the benefit of the industry—in this case physicians. The two organizations rapidly developed very strong links, which enabled each to serve the needs of the other while at the same time actively opposing alternative forms of health care organization such as health care cooperatives (Starr 1982, 309).

There was some marketing of private health insurance through the workplace as a benefit prior to World War II. However, during the war provision of health care benefits through the workplace increased dramatically because of a federal ruling that such benefits did not contribute to inflation (as did pay raises, for example). Management used health benefits to attract workers during the war-induced labor shortage:

> Blocked off from federal action, caught up in the spirit of national unity to win the war, confronted by a wage freeze, the labor movement had begun to look for more immediate relief. By the 1940s, the powerful industrial unions began to win hospital and medical coverage—ILGWU, Mine Workers, Amalgamated, UAW, UE, etc. Prevented by World War II from being able to improve the wage levels of their membership because of the wage freeze, the unions turned to "fringe benefits," establishing in lieu of wage increases "non-inflationary" paid holidays, vacations, pensions, hospital and medical benefits as part of their union contracts. (Riskin 1991)

Walter Reuther, as president of the United Auto Workers (UAW) during this period, played a special role in terms of national health care policy. After purging the UAW of its progressive leadership,

> now Reuther was free to further his own policies. While fringe benefits are paid for by the workers through wage offsets, not as gifts from the corporations, the very size of health care benefits costs severely undercuts needed wage increases. This fact was obscured in the tremendous publicity Reuther won for "winning" health care benefits from the auto corporations. . . . From this point on, the UAW formally supported health care legislation such as Kennedy introduced—but significantly all such legislative activity was linked to preserving the private insurance approach, thus undermining the central need for federal funding and administration, and guaranteeing profits instead of health care to everyone. While this approach won significant practical benefits for the workers [and] increased the prestige of their union leaders, it contained its own limitations:
>
> 1. It divided the labor movement from its allies;
> 2. It created rivalry and divisions among the unions, in which each tried to set the pace in separate negotiations;
> 3. It distracted from the united, national drive of all progressive forces for a common social goal;

4. It ignored the welfare of the rest of the population;
5. It set the foundation for the current national crisis enabling the private insurance companies and profit-making to create the present monstrous and costly maelstrom. (Riskin 1991)

After the war, health benefits became a major bargaining issue as a result of the burgeoning development of collective bargaining and the absence of national health insurance. By 1954 one-quarter of all purchased health insurance was negotiated through organized labor and covered a total of 29 million persons (Starr 1982, 311–313). This was one of several reasons that the growth of private commercial insurance took off at about the same time. The number of commercial insurers offering policies that covered hospital fees grew from 28 in 1942 to 101 by 1949. Life insurance companies, which had traditionally sold insurance in the group market, came to dominate the hospital insurance market because an increasing portion of the business at the time in the commercial sector was based on group sales. Casualty insurers, traditionally selling to individuals, lost market share to the life insurance companies (Starr 1982, 328).

Needs of the Elderly and Needs of the American Hospital Association

During the late 1950s and early 1960s the health care needs of the elderly received a great deal of media and legislative attention. There was unprecedented popular support for national health insurance. Medicare, which was the politically compromised end result signed into law in 1965, met the needs of the health care providers better, perhaps, than the needs of the elderly. Following great success in eliminating legislated controls over reimbursement for services, the American Medical Association and the American Hospital Association won maximum control over operation of the program as a whole:

> Under Part A of Medicare, the law allowed groups of hospitals, extended care facilities, and home health agencies the option of nominating "fiscal intermediaries," instead of dealing directly with the Social Security Administration. . . . As expected, the overwhelming majority of hospitals and other institutions nominated Blue Cross. Under Part B, the secretary of HEW was to choose private insurance agents called "carriers" to serve the same function in a geographical area. The majority of these carriers turned out to be Blue Shield plans. As a result, the administration of Medicare was lodged in the private insurance systems originally established to suit provider interests. And the federal government surrendered direct control of the program and its costs. (Starr 1982, 375)

Health care costs escalated rapidly during the 1960s and 1970s, especially after passage of Medicare. The share of health care expenditures paid by insurers rose from 45 percent to 67 percent from 1960 to 1975. "Third-party, fee-for-service payment was the central mechanism of medical inflation" (Starr 1982, 385). Despite the burgeoning costs, huge gaps in coverage remained that neither the public nor private sectors were addressing. In addition it became more clear to labor that increasingly expensive health care benefits were displacing wage raises and other benefits.

At the end of the 1960s the call for a comprehensive national health insurance plan arose once again, this time led by Walter Reuther, president of the United Auto Workers. He began organizing the Committee for National Health Insurance. At the same time, the American Federation of Labor and Congress of Industrial Organizations (AFL-CIO) Social Security Department developed its own national health insurance program. Popular support was so strong for the concept that rather than fight it head on, the insurance industry, the AMA, and the AHA proposed alternative plans. "Reflecting this new development in 1967, Senator Edward Kennedy (D-Mass.) introduced the first version of a long series of health care bills, winning wide support from the AFL-CIO, its major unions, from progressive forces generally, and from some of the largest and most active senior organizations" (Riskin 1991).

In general Kennedy's proposed legislation would have nationalized health insurance but left all health services in the private sector. The Republican administration's response was to blunt the movement for national health insurance by funding seed money for a national program of health maintenance organizations (HMOs), prepaid group practices that health care providers and the commercial health insurance industry could live with. In addition, during the 1970s watered-down versions of Kennedy's original bill were proposed, only to be rejected by organized labor and other activists who supported the original version. Finally, "the combined impact of recession and inflation hopelessly stalled the movement for national health insurance after 1974" (Starr 1982, 406).

Medical Committee for Human Rights

The Medical Committee for Human Rights was composed of health activists in the 1960s and early 1970s. They negotiated with Rep. Ron Dellums (D-Calif.) to introduce legislation for a national health *service* (in contrast to national health *insurance*). The Committee for a National Health Service was formed in 1975 to develop the legislation and the political backing for it. The U.S. Health Service Act was first introduced a couple of years after that. The act calls for a federally funded, locally controlled health care system operated as a public service with no private

TABLE 2.1 Benefit Expenditures of Private Health Insurance Organizations, 1970–1987 (in millions of dollars)

	1970		*1980*		*1987*	
	Amount	*% of Total*	*Amount*	*% of Total*	*Amount*	*% of Total*
Blue Cross/Blue Shield	7,060	46	25,467	38	44,525	32
Commercial insurance	7,104	46	25,774	38	51,549	37
Independent plans	1,156	8	16,264	24	43,016	31

Source: U.S. Department of Commerce, Bureau of Census, *Statistical Abstract of the United States, 1990* (Washington, D.C.: GPO, 1990), p. 95.

health insurers involved and no profit-making health care providers included. All health care would be available at no charge to residents of the United States. Later the committee was renamed Coalition for a National Health Service and in the mid-1980s was renamed a third time—Coalition for a National Health System. Coalition members have included major national organizations such as "the American Public Health Association, the National Association of Social Workers, the American Student Medical Association, the National Women's Health Network, and the national Gray Panthers" (Danielson and Mazer 1986).

In the 1980s the Reagan administration's devastating attack on social services forced health care reformers into a defensive struggle. Health care activists focused increasingly at the state level, where political resistance was judged to be less monolithic than at the federal level.

Economic Profile of the Health Insurance Industry

Table 2.1 summarizes benefit expenditures of private health insurance organizations during the period 1970–1987. This comparative measure is a reasonable indication of market share held by each of the three categories of private health insurers. In 1970 commercial insurers and the Blues (as Blue Cross/Blue Shield organizations are popularly called) each paid about 46 percent of all health benefits. Independent plans, typically self-insured enterprises, paid about 8 percent of all private health benefits. During the subsequent seventeen-year period independent plans steadily gobbled up market share. Larger companies have increasingly self-insured because of numerous economic advantages over purchasing plans from the commercial insurers. By 1987 self-insurers were paying nearly one-third of all private health insurance claims. Approximately 80 percent of the Fortune 500 companies self-insure

(Fraser 1990). Although both the commercial insurers and the Blues consistently lost market share to the independent plans, the Blues lost significantly more compared with the commercial insurers. The former dropped to 32 percent, whereas the latter dropped to 37 percent of total private health benefits paid. This trend has resulted in large part from the "cream skimming" systematically practiced by commercial insurers. They have marketed more aggressively to narrower, healthier populations and have been able to sell less expensive policies in some niches compared with the Blues. The Blues, however, are increasingly left with a "sicker" population that has to pay higher premiums. Historically the Blues have been somewhat less restrictive in terms of who they accept in their plans, although in recent years they have been tightening up in order to better compete with commercial insurers.

The commercial insurance industry, as distinct from the Blues and the self-insured, is typically split into two branches: property/casualty and life/health. The property/casualty side of the industry sells primarily liability insurance such as property, medical malpractice, automobile, home owners', commercial, fire, workers' compensation, and so on. The life/health side sells predominantly life and health insurance. There is some overlap. A number of large multiline companies have operations on both sides of the industry. The two branches of industry are further split into mutual companies and stock companies. Nominally a mutual company is owned by policyholders and managed by an elected board of directors. Profits are returned to policyholders in the form of policy dividends. A stock company is owned by its stockholders, who are also the recipients of profits. In actual practice, however, there is little difference in operation between these two types of companies in any other significant respect. Moreover, there appears to be a trend for mutuals to convert into stock companies in order to be able to sell stocks to raise capital (A. M. Best Lowers Equitable Life's Rating 1991; Goodfriend 1991; Equitable's Surplus Declines to $1.1 Billion 1991).

As detailed in Table 2.2, the commercial insurance industry as a whole has assets of $1.8 trillion, greater assets than several sectors of U.S. industry (U.S. Department of Commerce 1990, 492). The life/health side of the commercial insurance industry is the stronger of the two with two-and-a-half times the assets and nearly 18 percent more income from premiums in 1989 than the property/casualty side. The life/health branch of the commercial insurance industry overwhelmingly dominates the sale of health insurance. In 1989 it sold thirteen times more health insurance than the property/casualty side, representing nearly a quarter of all premiums taken in by the life/health branch of the industry. Compared with other forms of insurance, however, health insurance is not particularly profitable. On the life/health side of the industry, in 1989 health

TABLE 2.2 Selected Data for the Property/Casualty and Life/Health Branches of the Commercial Insurance Industry, 1989

	Property/Casualty	*Life/Health*
Admitted assets (000,000)	526,985	1,298,480
Total premiums written (000,000)	208,834	245,750
Accident and health premiums written (000,000)	4,594	59,742
Accident and health premiums as percentage of total premiums	2.2	24.3
Net gain before federal income taxes		
Accident and health (000,000)	114	2,114
All insurance lines (000,000)	17,265	14,045
Accident and health as percentage of all lines	.7	15.1

Sources: Best's Aggregates & Averages, Life-Health, 1990 (Oldwick, N.J.: A. M. Best Company, 1990), pp. 11, 40; *Best's Aggregates & Averages, Property-Casualty, 1990* (Oldwick, N.J.: A. M. Best Company, 1990), pp. 2, 64, 91, 124.

insurance accounted for nearly a quarter of the premiums but only about 15 percent of the profits.

In 1986 there were nearly 2,000 insurance carriers selling health insurance, often as one of several lines of insurance carried. They employed 164,000 people, who were predominantly associated with the health insurance business. These employees had an annual payroll of $4 billion and represented about 12 percent of all employees in the commercial insurance industry (U.S. Department of Commerce 1990, 490).

As discussed earlier, developments among the three sectors of private health insurance over the past couple of decades include the dramatic rise of independent plans and the simultaneous loss of market share by the commercials and even greater loss by the Blues. Changes in the health insurance arena that are equally dramatic take place when private health insurance as a whole is compared with public health insurance in the form of Medicare and Medicaid. By any measure the private sector of health insurance is steadily shrinking. As noted in Table 2.3, in 1970 private health insurance paid for 63 percent of all public and private health insurance benefits. By 1987 the proportion had dropped to 56 percent.

Table 2.4 concerns the declining role of private health insurance from the perspective of persons insured and uninsured rather than the proportions of benefits paid. The results are striking. From 1970 to 1987 the proportion of all persons in the United States enrolled in Medicare rose from 10 percent to 13.3 percent and the proportion of Medicaid recipients rose from 8.6 percent to 9.5 percent. During just the seven-year period

TABLE 2.3 Benefit Expenditures for Private Health Insurance, Medicare, and Medicaid, 1970–1987 (in millions of dollars)

	1970	*1980*	*1987*
Private health insurance organizations	15,320	67,504	139,090
Medicare and Medicaid	8,940	46,118	102,555
Private and government expenditures combined	24,260	113,622	241,645
Private as a percentage of combined	63	59	56

Source: U.S. Department of Commerce, Bureau of Census, *Statistical Abstract of the United States, 1990* (Washington, D.C.: GPO, 1990), p. 95.

TABLE 2.4 Number of Uninsured and Insured by Source of Insurance, 1970–1987

	1970	*1980*	*1987*
Total United States population (in millions)	205,052	227,757	243,934
Enrolled in Medicare (% of total population)	10.0	12.5	13.3
Medicaid recipients (% of total population)	8.6[a]	9.5	9.5
Uninsured (% of total population)	—[b]	12.6	15.2[c]
Privately insured[d] (% of total population)	85.5	75.3	74.2

[a]1972 data.
[b]Data unavailable.
[c]1986 data.
[d]Hospitalization insurance only, the most common form of health insurance. Column percentages do not total 100 percent because of overlapping types of insurance.

Sources: U.S. Department of Commerce, Bureau of Census, *Statistical Abstract of the United States, 1990* (Washington, D.C.: GPO, 1990), pp. 12–13, 100; Health Insurance Association of America, *Source Book of Health Insurance Data, 1989* (Washington, D.C.: Health Insurance Association of America, n.d.), pp. 32–33; Health Insurance Association of America, *Source Book of Health Insurance Data, 1981–2* (Washington, D.C.: Health Insurance Association of America, n.d.), p. 18; U.S. Department of Commerce, Bureau of the Census, *Historical Statistics of the United States, Colonial Times to 1970* (Washington, D.C.: GPO, 1975), p. 82; Patricia A. Butler, *Too Poor to Be Sick* (Washington, D.C.: American Public Health Association, 1988), p. 9.

of 1980 to 1987 the proportion of uninsured rose from 12.6 percent to 15.2 percent. During the seventeen-year period starting in 1970, however, the percentage of the total population with private hospitalization insurance dropped from 85.5 percent to 74.2 percent. During the eight-year period between 1980 and 1988 employment grew by more than 15 million, but during the same period of time there were 5 million fewer people covered by any private health insurance (Nadel 1991, 6). The private health insurance sector is increasingly unable or unwilling to insure American citizens. It has shoved tens of millions of people onto the rolls of public health insurance or, worse yet, into the abyss of the uninsured. Moreover, the trend continues.

Despite the fact that there are about 2,000 commercial life/health insurers, the industry is quite concentrated. The top twenty-five companies control 52 percent of the industry. In addition, the larger insurers are growing at the fastest rates. The top 100 life/health insurers control over three-quarters of the market and added more than $20 billion in new premiums in 1990 over the year before, an increase of more than 11 percent (100 Largest Life/Health Writers Dominate 1991). The decade of the 1990s will see substantial reorganization of the commercial insurance industry. Many companies, even very large ones, will fail. Mergers will further concentrate industry ownership and control into the hands of fewer and fewer corporate players. The health insurance industry may become even more unstable with the Chicago Board of Trade's decision to start offering health insurance futures contracts late in 1991 (CBOT Sets Oct. 1 Launch 1991). Remaining players will sell fewer types of insurance, thereby gaining an increasingly stronger hand in controlling selected markets. A number of major health insurers such as Aetna Life and Casualty and Travelers Corporation have stopped selling individual and/or small-business health insurance policies and have laid off or offered early retirement to thousands of employees (Berg 1991a). Some economists have warned that "the withdrawal from various markets by insurers will allow competitors to raise prices and leave an increasing number of people unable to find affordable insurance, forcing them into government-run insurance pools" (Berg 1991b).

The insurance industry is cyclical, with peaks and troughs occurring every few years. At the end of the 1980s the cycle appeared to begin an upswing, forestalling some of the anticipated business failures for a period of time. Health insurance premiums rose an average of 20 percent to 25 percent during 1989. This was the principal reason there was a 30 percent improvement in statutory earnings of the life/health insurance industry during the same period. This resulted in a very substantial 13.6 percent return on equity, that is, the rate of profit for the life/health insurance industry. In 1989 life/health profits were $10.4 billion, up 44 percent from four years earlier (L/H Industry New Operating Results 1990; 1989 Life/Health Year-End Financial Results 1990). In 1989 insurance stocks soared to their highest ever recorded levels. The A. M. Best (AMB) Life/Health Stock Index revealed that life/health insurance industry stocks gained 28 percent in 1989, the highest growth rate experienced by the index during the entire 1980s (Insurance Stock Trends 1990). However, in 1990 soured real estate holdings and the recession drove stock prices down 40 percent or more among several of the large multiline insurers; yet many of these stocks rebounded in the first half of 1991 (Laing 1990; Meakin 1991).

The Long-Term Care Market

According to industry analyst Ira H. Malis, vice-president of Alex. Brown & Sons, Inc., "The stocks of insurance companies with long-term care exposure have been among the best performers thus far in 1990. In our opinion, the outlook for the long-term care segment of the accident and health market presents the best growth prospects within the insurance industry in the 1990s" (Malis 1990).

By the end of 1989 approximately 1.5 million long-term care policies had been sold in the United States, but they represented only 5 percent of the potential market. In 1990 1.6 million policies were sold just in that year alone, representing a 26 percent increase over the previous year (Ferling 1991). Insurers are excited about the relevant demographics because senior citizens are the most rapidly growing sector of the population. The industry anticipates selling tens of millions of long-term care policies in the next couple of decades, and corporate moguls are dashing about even now to accomplish this task. In a 1990 nationwide survey of insurers by the National Association of Life Underwriters, sixty-five of ninety-seven respondents offer individual long-term care insurance policies and riders. This figure is up 20 percent over the previous year (Pullen 1990d). Unfortunately this sector of the health insurance industry also happens to be rife with fraud, corruption, and misrepresentation. There are likely to be millions of elderly victims of the insurance industry as the long-term care insurance sales blitz progresses.

Health Maintenance Organizations

Health maintenance organizations appear to have been going through a bit of a shakeout in recent years. HMO enrollments were up to 35 million by the beginning of 1990, but this rise represented a sluggish increase of less than 4 percent over the previous year. In addition the number of HMO plans shrank in 1989 to 623 from the previous year's 659. Some went out of business, whereas others were acquired. Hospital-owned HMOs shrank from 101 plans in 1988 to 85 in 1989. Independent plans lost ground also, declining in number from 148 in 1988 to 128 in 1989. Corporate owners are the big winners in the changing HMO market. Corporations dominated HMO ownership in forty states, up from thirty-four states in 1987 (Fewer HMOs Controlled by Hospitals 1990). Commercial insurance corporations in particular are purchasing a large proportion of HMOs. For example, in 1990 Aetna Life & Casualty agreed to shell out up to $34 million to purchase Partners National Health Plans, which is among the five largest health maintenance organizations in the United States (Aetna to Acquire 1990). CIGNA Healthplan, Inc., also ranks among the top five. Prudential recently expanded its HMO, PruCare, into the hot California market (California Still HMO Hotbed 1990). The Blues, emulating ever more closely their commercial life/health brethren, control the second-largest HMO affiliation in the United States (Arndt 1990b).

A study by a private research firm of HMOs nationwide found that HMOs had increased their premiums by nearly 17 percent in 1989 and 60 percent of the 371 HMOs that responded indicated that they had made a profit in 1989. One of the most frequent responses to a question regarding the reasons for making a profit in 1989 (apart from the obvious massive premium increases) was that unprofitable groups had been dropped from their plans (More HMOs Posted Profits 1990).

While HMOs are busy swelling the ranks of the uninsured by denying groups of people coverage, larger self-insured corporations are dropping HMOs that don't live up to corporate expectations. Late in 1990 General Motors Corporation ordered its employees not to enroll in nineteen HMOs and the corporation cancelled contracts entirely with six additional HMOs (Kenkel 1990b). Additional financial pressures on HMOs are forcing them to cut costs, often at the expense of their patients. HMOs nationwide have about ninety contracts with Medicare to provide medical services to 1.2 million seniors. The negotiated average rate raise for 1991 was a fraction of the anticipated inflation of medical costs. Because of variables in the complicated formula for applying the reimbursement schedules, some contracted HMOs will actually receive reduced reimbursements. A number of HMOs will shift rising health care costs to seniors in the form of increased deductibles or monthly fees (Kenkel 1990d).

A recent General Accounting Office (GAO) study of HMOs in Chicago with tens of thousands of Medicaid enrollees led to the conclusion that the HMOs "offered contractual incentives to physician subcontractors to limit utilization of medical services by Medicaid patients" (Study Hits HMOs' Contracts 1990, 12). In Maryland the attorney general warned physicians and other health care providers that it is illegal for them to bill HMO enrollees directly for services covered by insurance (Maryland Attorney General Warns 1990). Delayed billings may be the result of HMOs stalling payments to contracted health care providers in order to improve cash flow. Rather than taking it out on the patients, other providers are turning to HMO management. For example, some of the dentist and physician members of Bay State Health Care, the second-largest HMO in Massachusetts, are running their own slate of candidates in the upcoming HMO board elections. Providers claim that payments are insufficient, slow in arriving, or too frequently denied altogether (McGhee 1991).

Finally, competition over market share among HMOs and other health insurers often results in the addition rather than reduction of major costs. In Pennsylvania back in 1986 Blue Cross launched a $2.2 million advertising campaign aimed at selling its preferred provider plan over U.S. Healthcare's HMO. The HMO retaliated with a $1.3 million advertising campaign to sell its product over the other. These actions resulted in a bitter dispute involving suits and countersuits that alleged false and misleading statements. Independence Blue Cross will pay U.S. Healthcare, an HMO, $2 million to settle charges of libel in an advertising campaign. Although in this particular case the HMO "won," millions of dollars in litigation and advertising costs to gain market share will ultimately be shifted to the cost of health care for the insured under both plans (Philadelphia Blues to Pay 1990).

The Blues: Blue Cross and Blue Shield

In the big picture, as reported previously, the Blues have been losing out to independent plans, that is, self-insurers. Any company large enough to self-insure will very likely save money by doing so and will have more control over future costs. Also, the Blues have been losing market share to the commercial insurers who frequently undercut the Blues by cream skimming healthy populations and leaving the rest for the Blues or the public sector or simply leaving them uninsured. The Blues rapidly expanded their HMO operations in the mid-1980s. As a result, the Blues are currently the second-largest HMO affiliation in the United States. However, if the commercial insurers have not already outstripped them in aggregate HMO strength, they likely will soon. In 1989 the Blues HMO plans posted to reserves (i.e., "made a profit" in Blues-talk) $55 million after losing several times that the year before (Arndt 1990b). In 1990 the Blues HMO plans posted $200 million to reserves. Currently about one-quarter of all Blues health plans are managed care such as HMOs, but by 1995 the Blues expect that managed care plans will account for over one-half of all their health plans (Mulcahy 1991b).

> During 1988 and 1989, the [Blue Cross/Blue Shield] association increased its focus on cost containment and managing utilization of its HMO plans, while decreasing marketing of the plans, said Gary Meade, executive director of alternative delivery systems product performance for the asso-

> ciation. The HMO plans have focused on getting profitable versus marginal business during the past two years, Mr. Meade said. (Arndt 1990b)

Responding to market forces driven largely by commercial health insurers, the Blues have expanded into nontraditional services and organizational forms in order to capture or recapture portions of the changing market. Blue Cross/Blue Shield of Missouri, for example, recently acquired the second-largest third-party administrator of health care benefits in the state—Pension Associates. The Missouri Blues will now offer services such as administration and claims adjudication to self-insured businesses in the area (Missouri Blues Buys Pension Associates 1990).

Originally the Blues were established as nonprofit organizations with state charters directing them to provide health care services to the community, especially low- and middle-income groups. Over the years, however, about 15 percent of the seventy-three Blue Cross/Blue Shield plans nationwide have converted from nonprofit corporations into mutual insurance companies nominally owned by their policyholders. Although this kind of conversion may have helped the organizations become more profitable, the price was paid by policyholders. A recent request by Blue Cross/Blue Shield of Maryland to convert from a nonprofit to a mutual insurance company was rebuffed by the insurance commissioner because of the additional expense of millions of dollars annually that would have been charged to subscribers, subsidiaries, and associated self-insured plans (Md. Blue Cross/Blue Shield Loses 1991). A Blue Cross/Blue Shield plan failed in 1990—the first in more than half a century. This failure was another symptom of a disintegrating health care system nationwide. Until fall 1990 Blue Cross/Blue Shield of West Virginia, with well over a quarter-million beneficiaries, was the largest health insurer in the state. On October 2 the national Blue Cross/Blue Shield Association stripped the West Virginia plan of its license to use the Blue Cross/Blue Shield name and service marks. On October 11 the state insurance commissioner declared the plan insolvent, leaving $37 million worth of unpaid hospital and physician bills. Gaston Caperton, governor of West Virginia, told unpaid health care providers that they would have to absorb the losses because a special state regulation exempted the Blues from the state's guaranty fund, which would have otherwise fully or partially made up the losses. This special exemption is common across the nation for Blue Cross/Blue Shield organizations. It is not clear if state regulations will allow hospitals and physicians who are owed money by the defunct health insurer to bill policyholders. If so, policyholders who had purchased health insurance from the state's largest plan will then be liable to pay bills incurred during a period in which they were covered by the plan. There is little reason why this scenario could not be played out in coming years with other Blue Cross/Blue Shield plans across the nation (Kenkel 1990c; Kenkel 1990e).

Summary

From the 1940s through the 1960s, the private health insurance market was wide open for the commercial insurance companies and the Blues. Their extraordinary growth was predicated on medical underwriting for the commercials and regional monopolies for the Blues. Their very success, however, which promoted rapid cost increases in the 1970s and 1980s, laid the foundation for their emerging demise. The Blues lost significant market share to the commercials, and both have lost an enormous slice of the market to the self-insured. During the past couple of decades private insurers have lost millions of U.S. residents to the uninsured and to the publicly insured. The health insurance industry is in the middle of a process of significant and widespread restructuring.

chapter three

Creating the Uninsured

> **[Underwriting is the] process of examining, accepting, or rejecting insurance risks, and classifying those selected, in order to charge the proper premium for each. The purpose of underwriting is to spread the risk among a pool of insureds in a manner that is equitable for the insured and profitable for the insurer.**
>
> **—Dictionary of Insurance Terms**

There is no legal or de facto right to health care for U.S. citizens or residents. Rather, access to health care in the United States is principally determined by private insurers seeking to maximize profits by excluding coverage of "high-risk" unhealthy populations and insuring healthy "low-risk" populations who need a minimum of health care. The process of selecting which groups will be most profitable to insure and which groups will not is called "underwriting."

The related underwriting processes of rejecting insurance risks and charging the proper premium for those not rejected maximize profitability for the insurer while simultaneously wreaking havoc in the larger society. The underwriting principle of private insurance may be equitable for the insurer but not for tens of millions of people denied health care by the use of a principle intended to maximize profit rather than access. Nationwide reliance on the underwriting principle has created a vast army of uninsured.

The lack of health insurance has very real consequences concerning access to health care, quality of life, and the very question of life itself. Hundreds of thousands of critically ill uninsured persons are denied treatment every year at emergency rooms across the nation. Some have serious complications as a result of being dumped from an emergency room, and some die needlessly (Ansberry 1988). Even if admitted for hospital care, the uninsured are far less likely to receive standard medical diagnosis or treatment than those with adequate insurance. One study of more than 100 hospitals found that privately insured patients with cardiac problems were 80 percent more likely to receive a standard test for clogged arteries than the uninsured, 40 percent more likely to have coronary bypass surgery, and 28 percent more likely to have a specific procedure to enlarge diseased arteries (Angier 1990). Poverty and lack of health insurance combine to give the United States an extremely high infant mortality rate compared with other industrialized nations. In some low-income areas of the United States the infant mortality rate is actually rising (Nazario 1988).

Contrast the following fact with the balance of this chapter: Less than 1 percent of the elderly, those aged sixty-five years or more, lack health insurance (National Center for Health Services Research 1989). Rich or poor, white or minority, they have public health insurance. Medicare automatically covers nearly all persons sixty-five years of age or older. Despite its shortcomings, Medicare involves no private health insurance, no insurance profits, no excessive overhead costs, no medical underwriting, and no denial of coverage.

Who Are the Uninsured?

A recent study by the Census Bureau found that 63 million Americans lacked health insurance coverage for at least one month during a twenty-eight–month period beginning in 1985. This number of individuals was approximately a quarter of the nation's population during that period of time. Half of all young Americans between the ages of eighteen and twenty-four were not covered at some point during the twenty-eight–month period (Census Heightens National Health Insurance Issue 1991). At any given time there are about 37 million uninsured—about 15 percent of the U.S. population. The uninsured are not a random selection of citizens: They are concentrated in certain age, ethnic, and other social categories. These groups of people have been hurt the most by a health care system dominated by private health insurance.

The 1987 National Medical Expenditure Survey is the most recent comprehensive national survey profiling adversely impacted groups of Americans without health insurance (Short et al. 1989). Approximately 75 percent of all persons in families with a working adult had employment-related insurance. Given the importance of workplace health insurance, the major proximate factor determining the total number of uninsured persons was whether they were insured at the workplace: "Generally, those who were most likely to lack employment-related insurance included the self-employed and their families, part-time employees, persons employed in small establishments or drawing low wages, and those employed in industries characterized by seasonal or temporary employment" (Short et al. 1989, 10).

In 1987 nearly 29 percent of all uninsured persons were in families without a working adult. However, approximately 40 percent of all low-income employees earning $10,000 per year or less were not insured from either private or public sources. This group was hit particularly hard because public assistance programs like Medicaid do not cover most of the working poor. Some of the industries with especially high rates of uninsured, about double the national average, included agriculture, construction, personal services, and entertainment.

Uninsured Young Adults and Minorities

The 1987 survey indicated that over 30 percent of all young adults between the ages of nineteen and twenty-four were uninsured by public or private sources; this is the largest percentage of any age group. Separated and single persons were more than twice as likely to be uninsured than married persons, and divorced persons were nearly twice as likely to be uninsured than married persons. People living in the South and West were about 1.7 times more likely to be uninsured than persons living in the Northeast or Midwest because of a higher likelihood of employment-related health insurance in the Northeast and Midwest. Largely because of an employment pattern with fewer fringe benefits than those for whites, blacks were nearly twice as likely to be uninsured as whites, and Hispanics were nearly 2.5 times as likely to be uninsured as whites. The American Medical Association's Council on Ethical and Judicial Affairs recently released a report reviewing a number of studies that indicated that the health care of African-Americans and other minorities is inferior to that of whites. Minorities get less-frequent and less-aggressive treatment than whites. Their infant mortality is higher and their lives are shorter. A major contributing factor is that minorities are disproportionally uninsured (Report Cites Racial Discrepancies 1990).

Because these groups of uninsured people varied dramatically in size, distribution of the actual numbers of uninsured varied quite a bit from the groups at highest risk. For example, there were more uninsured married persons than any other marital status category and there were several times more uninsured whites than blacks or Hispanics. Although young adults were at highest risk to be uninsured, nearly a third of all uninsured were children eighteen or under—the largest number of uninsured in any age group.

The plight of approximately 10 million uninsured women of child-bearing age and the more than 11 million uninsured children in the United States is particularly tragic. According to congressional testimony by Dana Hughes, assistant director for state and local affairs of the

Children's Defense Fund, in 1986 almost one of five children living in families (as opposed to institutions) was completely uninsured (U.S. Congress 1989c). The proportion of children covered by employment-related insurance and private insurance from any source has been declining in recent years.

Children, Race, and Income

Family income is a major determinant of whether children are insured. In 1986 almost a third of the children who lived in families with incomes less than the federal poverty level were completely uninsured and 28.7 percent of the children living in families with incomes between 100 percent and 200 percent of federal poverty level were uninsured. An extraordinary 42 percent of children in poor working families were uninsured in 1986 because of declining availability of work-related health insurance and strict Medicaid eligibility provisions. Compare these percentages of uninsured children with the aggregate figure of 18 percent of children in families of all income levels who were uninsured in 1986. Nearly all the growth of the uninsured during the 1980s has been the result of shrinking coverage of dependents by employer-based insurance.

Race is also an important determinant of uninsured children. At every income level African-American children are more likely to be entirely uninsured than white children. In 1986 three of every ten African-American children in families with at least one employed adult were uninsured.

Income and race are also principal determinants of the insurance coverage of women of childbearing age. In 1985, 17 percent of all women ages fifteen to forty-four, a total of about 9.5 million women, had no health insurance of any kind. Another 4.5 million women had health insurance policies that did not cover maternity care. As a result, fully 25 percent of all women of childbearing age had no maternity care coverage. Unemployed women, and those working in low-paying jobs, were most likely to be uninsured. In addition, African-American women were more likely to be uninsured than white women. Low-income women who lack health insurance are twice as likely as insured women to receive late or no prenatal care, which is associated with much higher infant mortality rates.

Finally, even those covered by health insurance may find themselves in a situation similar to those with no health insurance. Depending on the insurance policy provisions, insured persons may be required to spend large sums of money out of pocket or forgo medical treatment altogether. A 1984 study by the Department of Health and Human Services, for example, found that approximately 60 million persons under age sixty-five with obviously inadequate private health insurance would have had the burden of unlimited medical expenses if they had experienced a major accident or illness. The study also found that in excess of 2 million families annually are forced to pay at least $3,000 in medical bills not covered by health insurance (U.S. Congress 1989e). These serious social impacts result from a number of common elements in health insurance policies. First-dollar deductibles may require the insured to pay out hundreds, even thousands of dollars each year before health insurance benefits kick in. Coinsurance rates often require the insured person to pay cash for a portion of covered claims. The typical portion paid in cash used to be 20 percent. New "low-cost" policies are now pushing up the coinsurance rates to 30 percent and even 50 percent for so-called budget insurance policies. There may be an annual upper limit on these coinsurance payments, but the limits vary considerably by policy. There may be limits to benefits paid on the type or number of selected insured services, and there may be total annual or lifetime limits that the insurer will pay on the policy (U.S. Congress 1988e).

Production of the Uninsured

The uninsured are produced by the health insurance marketplace. Ultimately, premium pricing and the rejection process of underwriting are the most important factors in the production and continued existence of the uninsured.

Medical Underwriting

Medical underwriting is the procedure used by health insurers to determine under what conditions individual coverage (in contrast to group coverage) might be approved or denied. Medical underwriting of individual employees is increasingly being used to determine the conditions under which small businesses will be insured or denied insurance or the conditions under which some employees within small businesses will be denied health insurance or denied full coverage that is provided to other employees. Medical underwriting is normally accomplished on the basis of medical questionnaires, physician evaluations, and/or medical testing. In contrast, larger enterprises are typically subjected to an "experience rating" procedure by commercial insurers to determine the conditions of group coverage. The prior claims experience of the company as a whole (i.e., cost of benefits paid out by the insurer) is used as the basis to set premiums for the next period, usually a year. Experience rating a business as a whole generally precludes medical underwriting of individual employees within that particular company.

In 1987 the federal Office of Technology Assessment conducted a survey of major commercial insurers, Blue Cross/Blue Shield plans, and health maintenance organizations across the nation (U.S. Congress 1988f). Despite the fact that the survey was conducted primarily to determine how health insurers were dealing with AIDS (acquired immune deficiency syndrome), a large amount of information was gathered about the more general practice of medical testing by health insurers. The results are pertinent primarily to those covered by individual rather than group policies. At that time about 9.3 million individual health insurance policies, which often covered dependents as well, had been sold by commercial insurers; 4.2 million individual policies were insured by the Blues; and about 1 million individual policies were insured by HMOs.

> Approximately three-quarters of individual and small group applications for commercial health insurance were classified as "standard" by the responding insurers and obtained coverage without extra premiums or special limitations. Twenty percent of individuals and 15 percent of small group members were rated as "substandard" and issued policies that exclude preexisting medical conditions, had a higher than standard premium, or both. The exclusion may be for a specific condition such as gallstones, or for an entire organ system, such as reproductive disorders. Finally, 8 percent of individual and 10 percent of small group applications were judged uninsurable and denied coverage. Most serious diseases were uninsurable, including severe obesity, diabetes mellitus, emphysema, alcoholism, coronary artery disease, cancer, schizophrenia, and AIDS.
>
> Risk classification by the responding BC/BS plans was similar to the commercial approach except for four "open enrollment" plans that accepted all applicants regardless of health status. The respondents accepted 83 percent of individual applicants as standard, 9 percent with substandard policies, and denied coverage altogether to 8 percent. Sixty to 100 percent of small group applicants were also accepted as standard by half the plans and up to 25 percent were denied.
>
> HMO risk classification differed from the others. Federally qualified plans are restricted to either accepting applicants at a community rate or denying membership altogether. As a result, exclusion waivers and substandard premiums are not common. The responding HMOs, however, were no more willing to underwrite high-risk applicants than the commercial insurers or BC/BS plans. They accepted 73 percent on a standard basis and denied membership to 24 percent of individual applicants. (U.S. Congress 1988f, 8)

In addition to ill health, factors commonly mentioned by commercial insurers that adversely affect an individual health insurance policy for an individual and dependents include financial status, drug abuse, occupation, suspected criminal association, and unethical behavior. A significant number of commercial insurers denied applicants if they lived in areas characterized as high in insurance claims or insurance fraud. Eighteen insurers, controlling about 10 percent of the individual market in commercial health insurance, considered sexual orientation in underwriting. Five of these insurers were among the largest twenty-five in the nation. HMO membership access was limited by many of the same criteria used by the commercial insurers. In contrast to commercial insurers and HMOs, however, insurability by Blue Cross/Blue Shield was almost entirely a question of health status. The major exception was that nearly half the Blues plans denied individual applications because of alcohol or drug abuse.

In an important ruling by the Pennsylvania Commonwealth Court that upheld a decision of state insurance commissioner Constance B. Foster, it is discriminatory when health insurers deny coverage to individuals for medical reasons in small group plans. Medical underwriting can still be used in Pennsylvania, however, to determine whether the small group will be insured at all and to attach exclusions for preexisting diseases (Pa. Regulator Upheld on Small Groups 1991).

Medical and Genetic Testing

Medical testing is commonly used by private insurance carriers to determine who has or may be predisposed to a wide range of serious diseases. The insurers' interest in knowing this information is not to help improve the health of the person being tested, but rather to avoid insuring and paying for treatment of the suspected medical problems or to avoid insuring the person altogether. Several dozen blood and urine tests are typically used by insurers to look for evidence of a wide range of diseases, disorders, and other types of information. These tests, for example, may be used to find evidence of kidney disease, bladder injury, diabetes, hyperthyroidism, liver disease, pancreatic cancer, anemia, heart disease, AIDS, and so on. Insurers may also require tests to screen for drug abuse and even for compliance with physician-ordered medication. In the latter case, insurers may want to know if the patient is complying with physician directions for taking required medication or they may want to see if the applicant is taking medication for a medical condition not reported on the application. Nicotine testing by insurers is used quite commonly for determining the possible eligibility of nonsmokers for discounts.

The use of medical testing results by insurers to exclude medical conditions from coverage and to deny applications for health insurance may have a significant arbitrary aspect to it. National studies indicate that laboratories vary tremendously in the quality of their work and the uniformity of results they achieve. Furthermore, false positives and false negatives are pervasive in the field of medical testing. In other words, the results of medical testing are often incorrect. For example, of every 100 positives indicated by a common test for colon cancer (carcinoembryonic antigen [CEA]), only 12 of the 100 people with positive results actually have the disease (U.S. Congress 1988f).

The evolving technology of genetic testing will likely provide insurers with a greater range of information about a person's predisposition to disease. This information will help insurance companies determine additional coverage to exclude and additional persons to deny insurance altogether. There is currently some evidence, for example, that genetic factors may influence the development of diabetes, mental illness, heart disease, and cancer. Even if insurers do not require specific genetic testing in the near future as part of their medical underwriting process, genetic test results will become increasingly available to them as part of the medical records of applicants who have undergone such testing independently. A recent study by a group of researchers from the Harvard Medical School surveyed incidents of discrimination based on genetic status. They found that insurers frequently considered the mere presence of a genetic trait or condition the same as a disability, even if the person with the genetic trait or condition had no clinical illnesses (Council for Responsible Genetics 1990). In summary, the greatest social impact of the increasing use of ever more sophisticated medical testing by the private insurers

> is likely to occur in the following areas: declining to provide insurance to those at very high risk, charging higher premiums for higher-risk applicants, and issuing policies with certain diseases excluded from coverage. These practices will aggravate what are already well recognized shortcomings in our nation's health care system: (1) the problem of the uninsured and underinsured, and (2) inadequate catastrophic and long-term health care coverage. (U.S. Congress 1988f, 21)

All states nominally regulate the insurance industry in general and hence the health insurance industry in particular. Often states prohibit certain discriminatory practices that may be related to medical testing such as issuing, continuing, or canceling insurance policies. As of 1988, Arizona, for example, had underwriting guidelines designed to protect against discrimination. Insurers are barred from asking questions about sexual preference, AIDS-related tests or exposure, life-style, or the receipt of blood transfusions. Typically, states that have tried to implement this type of antidiscriminatory legislation have faced very strong challenges by the insurance industry. In some cases these contests have resulted in court-invalidated antidiscrimination regulations (Council for Responsible Genetics 1990). In Florida, coverage containing exclusionary language that bars coverage for a specific disease may not be written. In Washington, a regulation requires that medical testing have a high degree of accuracy before it can be used to deny insurance to an applicant or charge the applicant higher-than-standard rates. Some states prohibit charging higher premiums on the exclusive basis of certain physical conditions. Larger firms that self-insure rather than purchase third-party private insurance do not fall under state regulation of the insurance industry because of federal exemption. As a result, a large portion of the work force and their dependents may not be afforded the minimal protection that is provided to other populations insured by regulated third-party insurers (U.S. Congress 1988f).

AIDS

In 1990 commercial life and health insurers estimate that they paid out $1.2 billion in AIDS-related claims. This total amounted to 3.5 percent of the claims paid to persons with individual policies and less than 2 percent of the claims paid for group health policies (Piller 1991). Nevertheless, insurers will not knowingly insure persons with AIDS or persons they believe are likely to get AIDS. According to a 1987 study by the Office of Technology Assessment, forty-one of seventy-three major commercial health insurance companies that responded to their survey screened for HIV (human immunodeficiency virus) infection (associated with AIDS) among applicants for individual policies and another ten insurers planned to do so (U.S. Congress 1988f). The seventy-three commercial health insurance carriers represented 57 percent of the commercial individual health insurance market. Admitting AIDS, AIDS-related complex (ARC), or an HIV-positive lab test on a medical history questionnaire resulted in immediate denial of the application. A physician's statement verifying any of the above would also result in immediate denial of the application. Knowingly misrepresenting these findings on an application would probably result in the insurer denying reimbursement for the condition or terminating coverage entirely. In some states HIV testing is prohibited to prevent discrimination against HIV-positive persons. Seventeen insurers in those locations required a substitute test (T-cell subset study), which they used to circumvent the ban on HIV testing. HMO and Blue Cross/Blue Shield screening for AIDS and related diseases does not appear to differ markedly from that of the commercial insurers.

In a recent example of an alleged AIDS-related discrimination lawsuit, Great Republic Insurance Company of Santa Barbara, California, was accused of discriminating against homosexual men by attempting to refuse insurance to applicants who, in the company's opinion, were gay. The plaintiff was a single male who was denied a policy after refusing to answer a supplemental questionnaire the company required of single male applicants who had jobs that did not require physical exertion and who had no dependents:

> Under the settlement agreement, Great Republic is barred from using the supplemental questionnaire to target single men, and is prohibited from using sexual orientation in the determination of insurability. The company also cannot use marital status, "living arrangements," occupation, gender, medical history, beneficiary designation, zip code or identity of the insurance agent to establish, or aid in establishing, the sexual orientation of any applicant. (Great Republic Agrees to Settle 1990)

Great Republic agreed to pay the plaintiff $85,000 as part of the settlement. In the judgment of the insurer, Great Republic had been "exposed to the allegation that [Great Republic] discriminated against gays simply because the two groups (gays and persons with AIDS) overlap to such a large extent" (Great Republic Agrees to Settle 1990).

In another important recent AIDS discrimination case the nonprofit community service AIDS Project Los Angeles won nearly $900,000 in damages. Bayly, Martin & Fay of Los Angeles had allegedly agreed to provide health care coverage to the AIDS Project but then backed out of the agreement a few days later when another broker told them that a number of Project employees either had AIDS or tested HIV positive (Haggerty 1991).

Insurers Fight to Allow AIDS Discrimination

As of the beginning of 1991 California was the only state prohibiting the use of AIDS tests results by insurers. In other states coordinated lobbying or court challenges by the insurance industry have prevented legislation or regulations with a similar goal. In New York, for example, Governor Mario Cuomo proposed legislation to prohibit health insurers from ordering HIV testing, but it failed in the legislature in 1986. The next year the New York Department of Insurance Administration promulgated a regulation with the same purpose, but it was challenged in court by a slew of health insurers. Ultimately the New York Court of Appeals ruled in December 1990 that health insurers are allowed to test applicants for the HIV virus and can deny coverage to applicants based on those tests (N.Y. Court Permits AIDS Testing 1990). In Hawaii, despite strenuous opposition by the state health director John Lewin, state insurance commissioner Robin Campaniano recently ruled that insurance companies can use the results of HIV testing as long as all enrollees are tested. Director Lewin opposed the new rules on the basis that HIV tests would be used to deny coverage to people with HIV (Hawaii Health Director Criticizes 1990).

The Home Office Reference Laboratory, Inc., is the major medical testing lab used by the life and health insurance industry. In 1986 this lab conducted 128,000 tests to determine the presence of antibodies to the AIDS virus, which indicates the presence of the AIDS virus. In addition, the lab conducted 25,000 T-cell tests to determine immune function status, a test typically given by insurers attempting to circumvent the prohibition in some states on more direct tests that indicate the presence of AIDS. Researchers who conducted the Office of Technology Assessment study of health insurer medical testing estimated that approximately 70 percent of the persons who received blood testing at the Reference Laboratory were also tested for presence of the AIDS virus (U.S. Congress 1988f).

The obstacles to obtaining private health insurance coverage are likely to grow for those with AIDS or with life-styles or personal medical histories likely to lead to AIDS infection in the opinion of the private insurers:

> The commercials, BC/BS plans, and HMOs reported similar methods to reduce their exposure to the financial impact of AIDS. These activities included reducing exposure to individual and small group markets by tighter underwriting guidelines, expanding the use of HIV and other testing, adding AIDS questions to the enrollment applications, and denying applicants with a history of sexually transmitted diseases. Two commercial insurers intended to place dollar limits on AIDS coverage in new policies, and one was introducing a waiting period for AIDS benefits. One HMO intended to withdraw from the individual health insurance market altogether, and a commercial carrier reported withdrawing from the District of Columbia. A BC/BS plan intended to lengthen the waiting period for new subscribers with a history of hepatitis, lymph disease, and mononucleosis, and two others were expanding their AIDS education efforts. (U.S. Congress 1988f, 11–12)

Another serious obstacle to effective AIDS insurance coverage is found in the massive shift among large and medium-sized businesses to virtually unregulated self-insurance plans. For example, in a case involving the H & H Music Company of Houston, employee John McGann was diagnosed with AIDS late in 1987 and so informed his employer. A few months later H & H dumped its former group health insurance and adopted a self-insured plan. Under the old plan as much as $1 million in lifetime benefits were available to an employee with AIDS. Under the new plan AIDS benefits were capped at $5,000. McGann sued H & H, the plan administrator, and the excess risk coverage insurer for discrimination under the federal Employee Retirement Income Security Act (ERISA). The U.S. district judge dismissed the lawsuit, ruling in effect that even if an employer knows about an employee's illness, under ERISA the employer can change or even terminate a medical plan. The case has been appealed, but this ruling seems to indicate that self-insured plans fall under ERISA regulation (or lack thereof) and employers in companies with self-insured plans do not have to abide by laws (present in about half the states) barring discrimination in employment because of AIDS (Marcus and Swasy 1990).

ACT-UP, the high profile AIDS activist group, appears to have no intention of letting commercial insurers discriminate against people with AIDS. In spring 1991 members of ACT-UP demonstrated in front of the joint offices of the Health Insurance Association of America and the American Council of Life Insurance. ACT-UP spokespersons derided the health insurance industry for denying health insurance to persons with AIDS while simultaneously fighting against a national health program that would provide medical care to victims of AIDS. In addition, the health care activists staged a "die-in" at the White House, complete with posters calling for a national health plan (Fisher 1991).

The almost universal discrimination by health insurers against persons with AIDS, or those considered at risk for AIDS, appears quite disproportional to its effect on health insurers. AIDS does, however, make a wonderful scapegoat for insurers to justify higher premiums and all sorts of restrictive practices. In recent years, less than 2 percent of all premiums taken in by the health insurers were paid out for claims relating to AIDS. Furthermore, a national survey of 146 chief actuaries of the largest life/health insurers indicated that less than 5 percent of them felt that the financial implications of AIDS on existing business were high risk. Over half the actuaries termed the financial impact of AIDS little or no risk, and six of every ten actuaries admitted that they had not even altered their mortality pricing to account for AIDS. Actuaries are insurance mathematicians: Their job is to compute risk. They believe that the increased risk to the financial stability of health insurers from AIDS is insignificant (Intindola 1991).

Changing Jobs

Changing jobs can be a frightening prospect for employees and/or dependents with health histories that might ultimately result in denial, exclusions, or excessive premiums charged by a new carrier. A national poll conducted by CBS and the *New York Times* in summer 1991 found that three of every ten respondents indicated that they or someone in their household have at some time continued in a job they wanted to leave in order to keep health benefits. This phenomenon has come to be known as "job lock" (Eckholm 1991).

The Consolidated Omnibus Budget Reconciliation Act of 1985 (COBRA) may provide a modicum of assistance in such a situation. Under most circumstances COBRA entitles an employee who has worked for a firm with twenty or more employees and his or her dependents to continue the same coverage by the former insurer for at least eighteen months. A major drawback is that the employee must pay 102 percent of the cost of the plan, including both the portion formerly paid by the employee plus the portion formerly paid by the employer. This can be prohibitively expensive. Furthermore, rights under COBRA are lost if the employee's former employer drops health insurance for all current employees or if the employee becomes insured under a new plan. COBRA coverage can be maintained as long as eighteen months for most people while the waiting period for an excluded preexisting medical condition is in effect. If COBRA coverage under the old policy ends, and the waiting period for the new policy is still in effect, the employee or dependent will simply not be covered.

A number of states have continuation legislation with COBRA-like rights for continuing the former employer's policy for varying lengths of time. Many states also have requirements that employers and/or insurance carriers must offer conversion policies to former employees who have lost COBRA benefits or to employees who have had their group insurance canceled. Such policies are typically inferior to the group policy they replace and are frequently quite expensive (The Crisis in Health Insurance 1990).

Preexisting Disease

> People who have medical problems, however minor, are second-class citizens in the world of health insurance. Virtually no commercial carriers and only a handful of Blue Cross/Blue Shield plans will sell policies to anyone who has had heart disease, internal cancer, diabetes, strokes, adrenal disorders, epilepsy, or ulcerative colitis. Treatment for alcohol and substance abuse, depression, or even visits to a marriage counselor can also mean a rejection. (The Crisis in Health Insurance 1990, 540 [Part 1, August])

Those who currently have or in the past have had medical conditions affecting a limited part of the body such as migraine headaches, varicose veins, or glaucoma may be forced to purchase health insurance hobbled by "exclusion riders." These riders bar coverage of the specified condition for part or all of the time the policy is in force. Those with medical conditions of a more general nature such as mild high blood pressure or obesity may obtain coverage but at a price 15 percent to 100 percent higher than the standard premium. Indications are that one-quarter to one-half of all health insurance policies carry exclusion riders or higher-than-standard premium rates. If for any reason a health insurer refuses an application for insurance coverage, that fact is recorded at a centralized industry data base in Boston for possible release to the next insurer who receives an application from the same person (The Crisis in Health Insurance 1990).

Major Illnesses

Bob Pollard started a small business in Newport Beach, California, in 1981. He bought a health insurance policy to cover his family and one employee for $300 per month. In 1983 Pollard's fifteen-year-old son developed Hodgkin's disease, a form of cancer. Extensive surgery, chemotherapy, and radiation treatment were required over a long period of time. The Pollards' health insurance premiums doubled and tripled. By 1989 their policy had skyrocketed to an annual rate of $87,000. Despite the exorbitant rate, the Pollards were afraid to drop the policy for fear that no other insurance company would take them because their son had a preexisting serious illness. Their insurer began to send mysterious notices that the premium payments were overdue despite that they had been sent well before the deadline. Late payment is grounds for cancellation of the policy. The Pollards began to send their checks by registered mail. The Pollards were able to renegotiate a new individual policy for their son, now twenty-one years old. The policy must be renewed every three months and can be dropped if any serious illness develops (Primeau 1990). The sequence of events experienced by the Pollards is not unusual for the holders of individual or small-business health insurance policies (The Crisis in Health Insurance 1990).

Small Businesses and Individuals

Insurance companies typically offer special low rates the first year or two to insure employees of small firms with about twenty-five employees. Within a year or two, however, as claims start to come in, insurers often dramatically raise the premiums as much as 200 percent. Meanwhile, employers and/or employees who have experienced serious health problems are stuck with the insurer, who is rapidly escalating their premium costs because they probably will not be able to find another insurer at any price. Further, there is always the possibility that the present insurer will not renew coverage, which may leave the entire organization uncovered and unable to find coverage. Insurers of small firms may refuse to insure individuals with serious (and even not so serious) preexisting health problems. In some cases the existence of just one or two such employees may be reason enough not to insure the entire firm. Individual employees with existing illness or who have dependents with existing illness may be forcibly stuck in their jobs indefinitely. They justifiably fear taking a new job because it could mean losing their current health insurance and being denied health insurance by the insurer at their new job (The Crisis in Health Insurance 1990).

The difficulties of small businesses and individuals looking for private commercial health insurance policies are compounded by a recent development in the industry. Health insurers are dumping small-business and individual lines of health insurance altogether, focusing on more profitable lines of group health insurance for medium-sized and large businesses. Aetna Life & Casualty Company, for example, of Hartford, Connecticut, announced in 1990 that it would stop selling all individual health insurance policies. These policies amounted to less than 1.5 percent of the company's annual premium income from all lines of insurance. About the same time, another large company, Travelers Insurance Company of Hartford, also announced that it would cease selling individual major medical policies (Aetna to Halt Individual Health Sales 1990). In addition, Great Republic Insurance Company of Santa Barbara, California, announced in 1990 that it canceled a health insurance plan that covered 14,000 California residents with individual and small-business health insurance policies. It produced $25 million annually in premiums but was said to be unprofitable (Great Republic Drops Health Plan 1990).

Fitness Penalties

Dr. Charles Sterling is the executive director of the Institute for Aerobics Research in Dallas, Texas. His message is that fitness will be a big deal in the decade of the 1990s. In a mid-1990 presentation at a New York City fitness symposium he was quoted as saying that within months "the insurance industry will offer substantial reductions to fit individuals who can pass special tests of cholesterol, back strength, blood sugar and blood pressure" (Insurance Break Foreseen for the Fit 1990). Dr. Sterling was right in substance but a little late in his timing. Insurers have been flinging sticks rather than carrots as a result of personal fitness and health conditions for some time. For example, U-Haul International, Inc., charges each employee up to $10 per paycheck for being overweight, underweight, or smoking.

S. Joe Vinson, director of benefits at Baker Hughes, Inc., a Houston-based oil equipment manufacturer, is quoted as saying quite frankly, "We want to penalize those who cost us more." Baker Hughes charges smoking employees an additional $10 per month for health insurance. Since 1989 Southern California Edison Company has been "reducing" employees' medical insurance premiums by $10 per month if they pass a series of medical tests. Of course this approach is no different than penalizing those who do not pass the tests. In any case employees and their dependents pay less for health insurance if they score within norms established for cholesterol, blood sugar, obesity, blood pressure, and carbon monoxide (an index of smoking behavior). About three-fifths of the 11,000 employees and dependents who took the series of tests were eligible for the lower cost insurance premiums. Another fifth failed to qualify for the reduced rates but got them anyway by agreeing to participate in a physician-supervised health improvement program (Bernstein 1990).

Summary

The uninsured and the underinsured are created by a system reliant on private health insurance acting as the gatekeeper to health care. It is a system characterized by institutionalized racism and sexism. Among the most severely impacted by this system are minorities and single female heads of households (as well as children and youth) and employees of small businesses. Medical underwriting transforms technological advances in genetic and medical testing from tools to promote public health into tools to deny access to health care. Finally, the cumulative social effect of market-driven private health insurance is to insure those who are least likely to need health care—and to overcharge, inadequately insure, or refuse to insure the rest.

chapter four

Employer Cost-Cutting Strategies

> **Employer-provided health insurance is eroding in the United States. Rapidly rising health care costs have impacted both insurers and employers. Competition among insurers has encouraged the use of practices that exclude some employees with potentially expensive health care costs. Competition among employers has caused some to eliminate or reduce health benefits for employees, dependents, or retirees.**
>
> ***—U.S. General Accounting Office 1990, 32***

General Accounting Office researchers reported that employer health costs totaled $15.3 billion in 1970 to cover their employees. The comparable cost climbed to $135 billion by 1987—nearly a 900 percent increase (U.S. General Accounting Office 1990). Expressed in another way, business health expenditures averaged 3.5 percent of wages and salaries in 1970 but well over 7 percent by 1987. According to national surveys of thousands of employers in 1988 and 1989, the cost of employee health insurance rose 20 percent each year (Health Care "Action Day" Set 1990; Employer Insurance Costs Jump 1990). A mid-1991 survey of fifteen top group health insurers revealed expected corporate health insurance renewal costs to increase 20 percent to 32 percent over the previous year (Medical Plan Costs 1991). These phenomenal rises in the cost of health insurance, several times the rate of inflation, have caused employers, often in collaboration with insurers, to pursue a variety of cost-cutting strategies.

According to a recent poll of businesses by the National Institute of Business Management, 88 percent of the respondents had adopted strategies to contain costs: "A sizable majority, 43%, increased employee deductibles, 16% raised employee paid premiums, and 16% shopped around for alternate suppliers. Other cost-saving maneuvers include:

shifting to HMOs and Preferred Provider Organizations (13%); preauthorization and self insurance, 9% each; cutting benefits, 4%. But less than half of those surveyed were satisfied by the results of the cost cutting" (Randall 1990, 7).

Cost Shifting

Between 1965 and 1980 there was a steady increase in the share of health care costs paid by business and government and a steady decline in the share paid by households. During the 1980s, however, the trend reversed itself. The household share of health care costs began to increase while government and business footed a smaller proportion of the health care bill (U.S. General Accounting Office 1990). The resulting increase in the household share of health care costs eliminated most of the real income growth for median-income households in the 1980s (Health Costs 1990). A large part of this massive shift in health care costs was a result of business-initiated cost-saving strategies targeting health insurance premiums. The outcome was a shift of health care costs to employees.

In 1980, for example, 74 percent of all employees covered by health insurance had that insurance fully paid by their employer. By 1988 the proportion of employees with fully paid coverage dropped dramatically to 55 percent. During the same period of time, fully paid family health insurance plans dropped from 54 percent to 37 percent and employee health insurance deductibles of $150 or more rose from less than 10 percent to about 40 percent. Just during the three years between 1986 and 1988 the average annual employee share of the cost of family health insurance premiums rose nearly 40 percent to $605. In addition, during that same period 20 percent more employers required that their employees pay for some portion of the family health insurance coverage. By shifting the cost of health insurance for family coverage to the worker, lower-income families are often forced to forgo health insurance coverage altogether (U.S. General Accounting Office 1990).

Retirees

In 1988 there were 7 million retirees and dependents covered by health insurance that was paid for all or in part by former employers for a total cost of $9 billion. In that same year total liabilities of U.S. corporations for future retiree health benefits were more than a quarter of a trillion dollars (U.S. General Accounting Office 1990). It is not surprising that corporations are investigating every conceivable way to reduce their financial burden, typically by increasing the burden on the retiree and his or her family. There are few legal obstacles to this cost-shifting strategy.

A current survey indicated that about 1 percent of the firms in the sample had recently dropped retiree benefits altogether and more than 40 percent had altered retiree health benefits in some form (U.S. General Accounting Office 1990). Many firms in recent years, for example, have shifted from defined benefit plans offering a certain level of care regardless of cost to a defined dollar contribution plan offering a fixed sum of money to be applied to health care benefits. The second plan shifts costs from the employer to the employee because the employee pays the difference between the actual cost of health care and the employer's cash contribution.

A survey of twenty-nine companies in the Chicago area was conducted recently by the General Accounting Office to determine changes in retiree health plans during the period 1984–1988. The GAO found that every company contacted had made cost-saving changes in their health plans, although not all the changes affected retirees. Typical changes included the addition of cost-containment measures, increasing deductibles and coinsurance provisions, and raising the employees' share of the plan cost.

> However, a few of these companies have made even more significant changes specifically to help limit retiree health costs. For example, one company has decided to phase out retiree health coverage altogether. Current employees and retirees will not be affected; new employees will not receive health benefits upon retirement. Another company will begin giving retirees a fixed dollar amount for health benefits in 1991. A third company eliminated dental benefits for retirees. (U.S. Congress 1990b, 37)

Employers also attempt to shift the cost of health insurance to the public sector. In May 1989 Illinois established the comprehensive health insurance plan (CHIP), a state-subsidized high-risk health insurance pool for persons unable to obtain health insurance on the private market. This high-risk pool is similar to others established in states across the nation. CHIP executive director Richard Carlson estimates that up to 10 percent of the limited CHIP policies have been bought by employees bounced from prior commercial policies. Their employers work with insurance agents to exploit a loophole in CHIP that results in lower commercial health insurance rates for employers who dump high-risk employees into CHIP. One employer was reported to have saved $30,000 a year in health insurance premiums by the systematic dumping of high-risk employees into CHIP (Jones 1990). In Washington, D.C., health insurance costs for the Whitman Walker Clinic are several times higher than for a typical comparable health plan because many of its employees have AIDS or the virus associated with it. The clinic is the major provider of health care services to AIDS patients. At the institution's request the city council passed legislation to heavily subsidize the cost of health insurance for clinic employees (D.C. City Council Approves 1990).

Plant closings and bankruptcies frequently result in the total loss of health insurance by retirees. Perhaps one of the most devastating cases of this occurred in July 1986 when LTV Corporation terminated all health insurance benefits for 80,000 retirees and dependents when it filed for Chapter 11 reorganization. Once retirees lose health insurance coverage it is typically difficult if not impossible for them to find new health insurance (U.S. Congress 1990b, 88).

Compounding all of these issues is a recent change by the Financial Accounting Standards Board (FASB) in required accounting practices of companies. The new regulation will require companies to report the amount of their unfunded liabilities for retiree health benefits on their financial statements. Previously most companies financed and accounted for retiree health expenses on a "pay-as-you-go" basis. In a statement to a congressional committee, Gregory McDonald, associate director, Income Security Issues, Human Resources Division, noted that "if all U.S. companies with retiree health plans were to begin advance funding their accrued liabilities of $296 billion, they would have to contribute an estimated $42 billion in 1991. This is about four times their 1991 [pay-as-you-go] costs of $11 billion" (McDonald 1991).

The rapidly escalating rise in the balance sheet expenses of many companies resulting from these required accounting changes may result in lowered stock prices or a reduced ability to raise capital. This will give management a very strong impetus to do what it can to reduce liabilities for retiree health care. Across the nation the result of this series of events will be the loss or reduction of retiree health coverage.

Reducing the Number of Those Covered

More than half the nation's employers screen job applicants for current or potential medical problems. Insurers are increasingly using preemployment medical screening to deny full or partial insurance coverage to employees despite federal and state laws that frequently prohibit the use of medical screening for these purposes (U.S. General Accounting Office 1990).

Nearly all firms employing 100 or more workers offer health insurance to at least some of their employees. Such firms employ about two-thirds of all nongovernment workers. At the same time, however, these same firms employ at least 38 percent of the working uninsured, or roughly three million employees (U.S. General Accounting Office 1990). A few of these uninsured work for larger firms that do not offer health insurance to any of their employees, but the vast majority of them are contingent workers, that is, contract, self-employed, temporary, or part-time workers. These contingent workers frequently are not offered company health insurance or cannot pay their share of it. At the same time, the contingent work force has been growing at twice the rate of the rest of the work force during the 1980s, in large part precisely because they are not offered health benefits and are therefore less expensive to hire.

Recently hired employees are experiencing increasingly longer waiting periods before they are offered health insurance benefits. Several years ago, for example, General Motors had a waiting period of only one to three months before a new employee could qualify for health benefits. As a cost-saving measure, that waiting period has now been extended to seven months. About 60 percent of all larger firms have waiting periods (U.S. General Accounting Office 1990).

Smaller firms are less well positioned to deal with the cost of rising health insurance premiums than larger firms, as discussed by Washington Post business writer, Jennifer Caspar: "Most major expenses hit a small business harder than a large one, but the high cost of insurance is twice as deadly because rates rise quickly and small companies do not have bargaining clout with insurance providers. John Galles, executive vice president of National Small Business United, said that premiums paid by small businesses average 40 percent higher than those paid by large firms" (Caspar 1990).

Small and medium-sized businesses, if they offer health insurance benefits at all, are more likely to be insured by a commercial insurer than they are to be self-insured. Approximately 30 percent of commercially insured businesses drop their insurers each year, usually as a result of price shopping for a better health insurance bargain. One reason the first year's health insurance policy is frequently much less expensive than subsequent years is that exclusions for the coverage of preexisting health problems among some of the employees expire (U.S. General Accounting Office 1990). The additional actual or expected health care costs result in higher premiums. As a result, frequent switching of health insurers may in fact save the employer money from reduced health insurance premiums the first year or two, but that is at the expense of employees who repeatedly get socked with preexisting condition exclusions time after time.

Reducing Benefits: "Low-Cost" Insurance

"Indeed," wrote Milt Freudenheim, noted health issues analyst for the *New York Times,* "the main backer of the stripped-down health plans is the insurance industry, which is trying to placate large employers, who resent having to pay for uninsured patients." He added, "The insurers are worried by the increasing support of employers and labor unions for more Federal regulation of health insurance as well as for a government-run system that could threaten the private insurance business" (Freudenheim 1990c, 1, 34[L]).

As of the end of 1990, eight states (Florida, Illinois, Kansas, Kentucky, Missouri, Rhode Island, Virginia, and Washington) have changed their laws to allow sales of cut-rate health insurance policies with relatively skimpy benefits. These policies are aimed principally at small business that do not or will not in the foreseeable future carry health insurance for employees because of the cost. The problem is real. In 1988, for example, health insurance premiums for employee benefits rose about 20 percent for large businesses with over 5,000 employees but rose an astounding 33 percent for small businesses with under 25 employees (U.S. General Accounting Office 1990).

The new policies sell for considerably less than standard group health insurance policies. The low-priced Blue Cross plan in Washington, for example, costs roughly half to three-quarters the full-priced policy. The average monthly premiums for a single person with a standard policy range from about $80 to $100 but only $60 for the cut-rate version. The average monthly premiums for a standard family policy range from $140 to $290, but only from $72 to $180 with the budget version (Freudenheim 1990c).

There are two main reasons these second-rate health insurance policies can be sold at lower cost to small businesses. The first is that they offer inferior benefits compared with standard policies. These policies provide reduced benefits because enabling legislation in the various states has exempted budget health insurance policies from state-mandated benefits that must be included in otherwise comparable health insurance policies. In Washington, for example, some of the mandated benefits excluded from second-rate policies include mental health care, mammography screening, and treatment for alcoholism and drug abuse (Freudenheim 1990c). Important benefit exclusions such as these typify cut-rate policies in most of the states. The second reason budget health insurance policies cost less is because a larger portion of the costs and risks are shifted from the insurer and the employer to the employee. In Washington the budget policy deductible is $500 per person, higher than many standard policies, and the copayment is 30 percent after deductible, 10 percent more than a typical policy (Freudenheim 1990c). In other words, the employee has to pay more up front for health care compared with a standard policy before the budget policy kicks in, and then he or she has to pay a higher copayment after it kicks in. A budget health insurance plan in Florida is being marketed with deductibles up to $1,000 and a coinsurance of 50 percent to some limit, for example $5,000, when full 100 percent coverage becomes available. In this plan the employee would pay 50 percent of all covered medical bills after paying a hefty deductible, before 100 percent coverage would kick in, which can cost up to several thousand dollars out of pocket each year. Premiums would be reduced 14 to 26 percent less than standard policies (Koco 1990).

Reducing Utilization of Health Care

Another range of strategies for both self-insured companies and those purchasing commercial health insurance coverage for employees involves reduction in the use of health care services, in contrast to reduction of the scope of coverage. Managed care programs typically include health maintenance organizations (HMOs), preferred provider organizations (PPOs), and utilization management fee-for-service plans.

> An *HMO* is a health insurer that directly provides or arranges for medical care for its members in return for a fixed per capita payment that is independent of the member's actual use of services. A *PPO* is an insurer that arranges for the provision of health services through a set of providers (hospital and physicians) that have contracted with fixed, usually reduced rates or fees. The contracting providers have agreed to be subject to utilization controls. Individuals who are insured by the PPO have a financial incentive to obtain their care from the contracting providers. A *managed fee-for-service insurance plan* pays providers a fee for each service provided, but includes provisions for prospective utilization review of these services. The purpose of such reviews may be to reduce either the number of hospital days or the cost for ambulatory services. (U.S. General Accounting Office 1990, 23)

Note that HMOs and PPOs compete against each other to some extent; however, HMOs are increasingly offering point-of-service options that give them the flexibility of PPOs. This option means that individuals who get medical care outside the HMO will receive lesser benefits than if they used the HMO network (Koco 1991). Managed care plans of all types have come to dominate private health insurance programs in the United States. Over 70 percent of all workers with job-related health care benefits were in a managed care plan in 1988. About 43 percent were in managed fee-for-service plans, 18 percent in HMOs, and 11 percent in PPOs (U.S. General Accounting Office 1990). Managed care plans are established in order to reduce employee utilization of health care services. This objective is the crux of the problem.

Employees with managed care plans are subject to a wide variety of obstacles to health care, such as HMOs with deliberately small parking lots and long waiting lists, managed fee-for-service plans with substantial fines for noncompliance with difficult admission review regulations, or physicians who are financially rewarded for providing the least amount of treatment possible. Some prepaid plans, for example, withhold 10 to 20 percent of the physician's fee as a backup for patient care costs that might exceed the budget (U.S. Congress 1989b).

Furthermore, HMOs and PPOs typically restrict employee choice of provider. Some larger companies are bringing back the less expensive "company doc," hired by the firm to see employees (Companies Being Forced to Share 1990). This strategy is even more restrictive of employee choice, obscures the independent role of the physician to ferret out occupational injury and illness, and may give the company de facto access to medical information that can be used against the employee. Finally, there are very serious questions about the quality of care that may be given in managed care situations and about the liability of the employer in a case where the quality or availability is poor (Mulcahy 1991a; Crosson 1991b).

Self-Insuring

Companies that self-insure rather than buy health insurance from commercial insurance companies have been growing at a phenomenal rate. One survey indicated that self-insured companies, typically large and medium-sized firms, grew from 20 percent in 1980 to 66 percent in 1988 (U.S. General Accounting Office 1990). There are a number of reasons employers like to self-insure. A principal reason is that much of the overhead of commercial insurers, such as profits and administrative costs, is eliminated. Furthermore, as a result of federal legislation, self-insured companies are exempted from nominal state regulation of rudimentary consumer safeguards like minimum standards of coverage and solvency of the insurance plan. Self-insured employers are also exempt from paying state insurance taxes and assessments, which are typically used to reimburse the victims of bankrupt insurance companies. They are exempt from having to contribute to state high-risk pools for those who cannot obtain health insurance from commercial insurers. Finally, the company rather than a commercial insurer is able to invest and profit from the pool of money set aside to pay health insurance claims. As a result of the self-insurance loopholes, employees in such plans may be more likely to receive inferior health insurance benefits from unregulated, financially shaky insurance plans.

Here is yet another reason for employees to be very wary of self-insured plans. A U.S. Supreme Court ruling late in 1990 strengthened the right of self-insured plans to operate outside the jurisdiction of state regulation of commercial health insurers. In this particular case the daughter of an employee of FMC Corporation was seriously injured in an auto accident. The family of the injured daughter won a cash settlement against the driver of a vehicle judged responsible for the accident. Self-insured FMC went after their employee's cash settlement to pay for some of the medical expenses the corporation had paid for the injured daughter. The court ruled that the state prohibition against commercial insurers seeking part of an insured's civil damages does not apply to self-insured companies (Ruling Exempts Self-Funded Plans 1990).

Summary

Employer health costs have burgeoned 900 percent between 1970 and 1987. Employees have suffered a long list of adverse consequences as a result of this dramatic escalation in employer costs. A large proportion of the increased costs have been shifted to employees through increased deductibles, higher employee-paid premiums, and a shift of the costs of dependent coverage from the employer to the employee. Employers are more frequently using preemployment medical screening to deny full or partial coverage for employees. There is also increasing use of longer waiting periods before medical benefits are available and increasing use of contingent workers with no benefits at all. The widespread use of unregulated self-insured plans increases the possibility that workers have below-standard benefits in a financially unsound system. Retirees have been hit particularly hard by employers who have shifted from defined benefit plans to defined-dollar contribution plans, increased deductibles and coinsurance provisions, raised the employee share of the plan cost, eliminated some types of coverage completely, or eliminated health insurance coverage altogether.

chapter five

Fraud and Deception

A recent Gallup Poll asked a nationwide sample of Americans how they would rate the honesty and ethical standards of people in a variety of occupational fields. Perhaps it comes as no surprise that members of the insurance industry were not rated very highly. In fact only people in advertising and automobile sales were rated lower. "We've seen these results in prior polls," noted Sean Mooney, vice-president of the Insurance Information Institute in New York, "but a lot of it depends on how the question is worded. I do agree, though, that the industry has an image problem" (Gallup Poll Blasts Insurance Industry 1990, 3).

The evidence, however, indicates that the insurance industry's image problem is firmly rooted in the public's very real experience with insurance fraud. For example, there is a wealth of data showing the strong and growing relationship between fraud and insurance company failures. A study by one of the leading insurance industry rating services, A. M. Best Co., determined that 80 percent of fraud-related insolvencies among property/casualty insurers since 1969 occurred during the seven-year period ending in 1990. A study by the American Council of Life Insurance that investigated sixty-eight life insurance company insolvencies during the period 1985–1989 determined that a quarter of them failed as a result of fraud and that fraud may have played a part in an additional 43 percent of the insolvencies. A study by the Texas Board of Insurance that examined thirty-four Texas insurance company failures from 1979 to 1990 found that 56 percent of these failures were fraud related (Lansner 1991).

Fraudulent Health Insurance Sales

Allegations of and indictments for fraudulent and misleading health insurance corporation activities are commonplace across the United States. A few examples reported during the first half of 1990 give an indication of the magnitude of the problem. In Texas, insurance commissioner A. W. Pogue recently issued an emergency cease-and-desist order to a number of California firms doing business in his state including United Healthcare Benefits Trust, United Association of Small Businesses, Inc., and United Health Insurance Administrators, Inc. The commissioner charged that these companies were unlicensed to conduct business in the state, that they employed unfair methods of competition, or that they engaged in unfair or deceptive practices (Texas Orders Health Insurer 1990).

A company based in Texas, Transport Life Insurance Company (a subsidiary of Primerica Corporation in New York), has been accused of selling expensive policies in New Jersey that paid out little to consumers. In addition, the policies were misrepresented as group insurance but actually had all the characteristics of individual policies. The New Jersey Department of Insurance threatened to fine the company $250,000, revoke its license, and issue an order to the firm to pay nearly $500,000 in unpaid medical bills. The Keith Wood Agency that actually sold the policies faces a $25,000 fine (Transport Life May Lose N.J. License 1990).

In the American heartland of Kansas the insurance department ordered an Arizona insurance firm and a Kansas insurance agency to stop using phrases such as "savings returned to you" and "benefits paid directly to you." The department charged that the use of such phrases may mislead consumers to believe that they will receive something other than a policy. Capitol American Life Insurance of Arizona and Inter-State Service insurance agency based in Kansas will share $125,000 in fines resulting from an investigation of their accident policy advertisements. This is the second time within a year that the state has taken action against the companies for misleading advertising practices (Advertising Claims Lead to Fines 1990).

On the West Coast the California Department of Insurance upgraded a prior temporary cease-and-desist order against Turks and Caicos Island–based Unified Assurance & Casualty. As of summer 1990 the owners and affiliates of Unified Assurance were permanently banned from transacting insurance in the state. It was found during a hearing that the firm was selling health and casualty insurance in the state without a license and was pursuing business in a "hazardous manner" (Calif. Takes Action 1990).

In another West Coast case, four Washington State–based insurers had been declared insolvent by mid-1989. However, it was not until the following year that they were barred from conducting business in Oregon. Western Timber Association, Western Business Association, Western Alliance of Agriculture, and Western Plans were charged by the Oregon insurance commissioner with conducting business illegally, misrepresenting financial reserves, and making profits three times as large as those authorized in the state. The firms had sold health insurance to about 1,000 Oregon residents (Four Washington-Based Insurers Barred 1990).

Angry Citizens

Angry citizens, consumer rights organizations, and consumer-oriented insurance commissioners are attempting to take fraudulent insurance companies to task. Current policy in Indiana, for example, permits the commissioner to fine fraudulent insurance companies or suspend or revoke a firm's license. Defrauded consumers, however, may lose their money even if the commissioner finds company wrongdoing and consumer compensation is warranted. One bill introduced in the General Assembly of Indiana early in 1990 would give the commissioner the ability to demand that an insurance firm pay a claim if the company were determined to have acted unfairly. Another bill would raise the maximum fine on unscrupulous insurers from $5,000 to $50,000 (Indiana Bills Would Increase 1990). A recent bill approved by the state senate of Louisiana mandates insurance firms that misrepresent policies or delay payment of claims to consumers for more than a month to pay special fines totaling $25,000 or four times the damage claim, whichever is greater (La. Bill Would Impose Special Damages 1990). The new Georgia insurance commissioner, Tim Ryles, has put together an insurance fraud unit replete with former FBI and IRS agents. Insurance fraud has recently been defined as a felony, and Commissioner Ryles is actively planning insurance sting operations based in part on consumer complaints to catch some of those felons. Fraudulent multiple employer welfare associations (MEWAs) will receive special attention (Knowles 1991b).

Florida seems to rank among the more militant states regarding attempts to control fraudulent insurers and agents. The insurance commissioner recently appointed Steve Burgess to a $60,000-a-year high-profile position as the new consumer advocate for health and automobile insurance. Burgess had worked in the Office of the Public Council for eleven years as a consumer advocate pitted against the state's Public Service Commission (Florida Insurance Consumer Advocate Named 1990). However, in a more controversial move, Florida insurance commissioner Tom Gallagher proposed fingerprinting all prospective insurance agents as part of the licensing process in order to facilitate a nationwide criminal check on each applicant. According to the commissioner, Florida insurance agent license applications currently request information about prior criminal records but a significant number of applicants lie about their backgrounds (Fla. Commissioner Wants to Fingerprint Agents 1990).

Special Victimization of the Elderly

Medigap Insurance

Approximately 29 million Americans over age sixty-five are covered by the federal Medicare health insurance program. Medicare, however, does not pay all the hospital and health care provider bills that an elderly person is likely to accumulate. There are substantial deductibles and coinsurance requirements that can add up to a large out-of-pocket sum for a senior citizen. As a result, at least 22 million seniors over sixty-five years of age currently pay out $16 billion a year to private medigap insurance companies to cover the gaps in Medicare (Freudenheim 1990b).

Medigap fraud, deception, and profiteering by the health insurance industry grew simultaneously with the development of the Medicare program. Congressional hearings in the late 1970s initially documented widespread exploitation of the elderly by the medigap insurance industry and resulted in passage of Public Law 96–265 in 1980, commonly referred to as the Baucus amendment, amending the Social Security Act. Nominally this bill was to establish minimum requirements for policies marketed specifically as medigap policies. The amendment set minimum loss ratio requirements (see following discussion), minimum benefits, and penalties for marketing abuses. The amendment was designed to encourage state regulation of medigap policies in accordance with federal standards.

This amendment, however, was extraordinarily weak and rarely enforced. It attempted to curb the rampant profiteering of the insurance industry by recommending that the industry have a goal of paying a minimum of $.60 in benefits for every dollar paid in premiums for individual medigap policies and a minimum of $.75 in benefits for every dollar paid in premiums for group medigap policies. In the insurance industry these ratios are known as "loss ratios." All things being equal, the higher the loss ratio, the better the deal for the insurance consumer. The recommended 75 percent loss ratio for group medigap policies is higher than the recommended 60 percent loss ratio for individual policies because there are fewer expenses involved in selling a group policy that covers a number of people than in selling policies to individuals one at a time.

The General Accounting Office (GAO) prepared a report toward the end of 1986 that evaluated the effectiveness of the Baucus amendment. Representative James Florio, chair of the Subcommittee on Commerce, Consumer Protection, and Competitiveness of the House Committee on Energy and Commerce, summarized the findings of the GAO study: "Fully one-third of the policies which they examined had loss ratios below the target of 60 percent. This meant that $650 million in premiums were paid by nearly 7 million senior citizens for policies which did not meet the 60 percent goal" (U.S. Congress 1988b, 1).

Incredibly, all these policies were "medigap approved" by the state or the federal government according to the provisions of the Baucus amendment. In other words, despite the Baucus amendment, profiteering by insurance companies and exploitation of seniors is still commonplace. During the same hearings in 1987 Congressman Claude Pepper testified that:

> In summary, the elderly today are no better off than they were in 1978, when my subcommittee first investigated medigap insurance. The only difference is the amount of money that seniors will waste to insurance ripoffs. In 1978, the subcommittee found that one out of every four dollars spent for medigap insurance by the elderly was wasted—about $1 billion. Today, more than $3 billion is wasted by older Americans annually. (U.S. Congress 1988b, 10)

In 1986 Blue Cross/Blue Shield sold about 45 percent of the medigap insurance, and commercial insurance companies sold most of the rest of it. Investigators for the Subcommittee on Health and Long-Term Care, House Select Committee on Aging, reported that most of the medigap abuse they encountered originated from smaller insurance firms specializing in selling medigap insurance rather than larger firms offering group policies (U.S. Congress 1986, 19). The subcommittee summarized a portion of their findings on abusive and fraudulent medigap policy sales in this manner:

> Abuses in the sale of health insurance to the elderly have been documented by the Congress, the States, local enforcement authorities and private consumer groups as early as 1965 when the State Special Committee on Aging conducted hearings into frauds against the elderly. . . . The most common abuses noted by regulatory authorities and consumer advocates from 1965 to present include the following:
>
> 1. Agents misrepresenting coverage or using brochures which indicate benefits which are not provided by the policy.
> 2. Agents recontacting long-time elderly insured and getting them to lapse policies to buy new ones.
> 3. Passing the names of elderly, sometimes senile customers, from agent to agent and thus causing the multiple sale of insurance policies.
> 4. Agents taking premiums for annual policies and having them issued on a quarterly basis to get [a] large commission.
> 5. Agents writing policies on sons, daughters, nephews, and nieces of elderly persons to avoid detection in their sale of duplicate policies.

6. Agents tearing out riders from policies before delivery to the insured. The riders are generally preexisting condition clauses which exclude payment for various health conditions the insured may possess for a certain time up to 3 years.
7. Agents using high pressure sales tactics or scare tactics to sell the elderly more insurance than they need. Sometimes several agents may visit an old person at the same time to multiply the pressure on the aged to buy insurance.
8. Agents forging the signatures of the insured on policies or applications. (U.S. Congress 1986, 55–56)

Routine Fraud and Misrepresentation

According to congressional testimony given by the American Association of Retired Persons, fraudulent and misleading marketing of medigap insurance has settled into several pernicious but fairly routine forms (U.S. Congress 1988b). Cold-lead advertising involves the direct mailing to seniors of official-looking mail, often with a Washington, D.C., return address. Recipients are invited to write for more information about purported changes in Medicare benefits or related information. The requested information may never be received, but the names and addresses of those responding are sold to insurance companies or agents who follow up with an unsolicited home visit.

Once an insurance agent is in the door, a new range of unscrupulous tactics may unfold. Because insurance agents receive a much higher commission on new sales than on renewals, they may pressure the current medigap policyholder to unnecessarily exchange their perfectly good current policy for a new one. This will probably leave the purchaser of the new policy unprotected during a new preexisting condition exclusion period or for other reasons often included in a new policy. Another tactic is to simply sell gullible seniors multiple redundant policies. Corporate management establishes a commission policy heavily weighted in favor of new sales in order to minimize the loss ratio (i.e., increase profits). As Earl Pomeroy, insurance commissioner of North Dakota, has pointed out:

> A management decision that can suppress loss ratios is to keep the business on the books for only a short period of time. We know loss ratios are incurred the older the pool of experience becomes. So they set a commission schedule for the agent that rewards the agent a very lucrative first-year commission for selling the product and a minimal renewal commission. The agent thus has a very strong financial incentive to put the business on the books and get it off the books before it's been renewed two or three times. (U.S. Congress 1988b, 62)

A GAO study conducted during 1989 and 1990 found that the widespread problems that had plagued the medigap insurance industry for two decades still existed. State regulation of medigap insurance, despite the Baucus amendment, varied considerably in scope and effectiveness. More than 4,400 complaints about medigap insurance were recorded in 1988 just in the ten states evaluated by the GAO study. Nearly $900 million in medigap premiums in 1988 paid for policies with substandard loss ratios. "Medigap-related complaints generally involved delays in paying claims or disputes about the amount of payments, poor service, premiums, marketing, coverage, or agents" (Medigap Insurance: Better Consumer Protection 1991, 16).

In summer 1990 a bipartisan collection of senators and representatives introduced federal legislation to correct "deceitful and fraudulent" medigap industry practices. The proposed legislation would require medigap insurers to get a signed statement from each potential client outlining all coverage that he or she already owned. Insurers selling redundant, unnecessary policies could be fined up to $25,000. In addition, the proposed legislation would require that medigap insurers pay out at least $.70 in benefits for every dollar in premiums they bring in, that there would be guaranteed renewability, and that there would be continuation of individual coverage upon termination of group coverage. Finally, the legislation would authorize $20 million in grants to the individual states to create counseling programs for those receiving Medicare benefits. The individual states would be responsible for enforcement in most cases (Legislation to Regulate Medigap 1990).

The health insurance industry was largely, but not entirely, pleased with this proposed legislation. A spokesperson for the Health Insurance Association of America (HIAA) noted that the proposed legislation was unnecessary because their 1989 national survey of seniors found that "only" 15 percent of those with private medigap coverage had multiple policies (Legislation to Regulate Medigap 1990). Apparently the survey failed to ascertain how many seniors had been sold multiple policies while being advised by insurance agents to let prior policies lapse. In any case, congressional legislation was enacted late in 1990 with provisions somewhat similar to those outlined earlier (Medigap Insurance Reform 1990). A history of lax state enforcement of long-term care insurance is reason to believe that the new legislation will not be much more effective than its 1980 predecessor.

Long-Term Care Insurance

Michael Hatch, commissioner of commerce for the State of Minnesota, has been quite candid about the value of much of the long-term care insurance sold by commercial insurance companies. At 1987 congressional hearings focused on regulating the insurance industry he asserted without reservation that "long-term nursing care is an absolute fraud in this country. The insurance being sold, an absolute fraud. Not a lot has been done to address that either" (U.S. Congress 1988a, 87).

Long-term care insurance is a very hot commodity in the insurance industry. According to industry analyst Ira Malis, vice-president of Alex Brown & Sons, Inc., "the outlook for the long-term care segment of the accident and health market presents the best growth prospects within the insurance industry in the 1990s" (Malis 1990). Nursing home expenditures are a $50 billion-a-year industry (U.S. Congress 1988d, 150). Currently nursing home costs average $25,000 to $35,000 per year and could easily increase to $50,000 per year by the year 2000. However, by 1990 only 1.5 million seniors had purchased commercial long-term care insurance to cover these overwhelming costs. This represents only about 5 percent of a potential market of seniors who might purchase private long-term care insurance. This potential market does not include about one-third of all seniors who are wealthy enough to pay cash or impoverished enough to qualify for Medicaid. Malis believes that 25 to 40 percent of the seniors in the potential market will have purchased commercial long-term care insurance by the end of the century. He neglected to mention that based on current practices millions of these seniors will also be defrauded or misled when they make their purchases.

In May 1987 the General Accounting Office released the results of a comprehensive nationwide study of long-term care insurance (in U.S. Congress 1988d). The research was conducted at the request of the late Representative Claude Pepper, then chair of the Subcommittee on Health and Long-Term Care, Select Committee on Aging. In a section entitled "Abuses in the Sale and Marketing of Long-Term Care Insurance" the GAO reported widespread unclear or complex policy language that resulted in consumer misunderstandings regarding coverage contents and limitations. In addition, the GAO found evidence of the same kinds of abuse and fraud encountered in the sale of medigap policies. These include "posing as a federal agent to sell policies, knowingly selling policies that duplicate the policy-holders' existing coverage, and selling supplemental policies by mail in states that have not approved their sale. . . . In addition AARP [American Association of Retired Persons] officials report that it is not unusual for insurance sales agents to falsely claim that AARP endorses their products" (U.S. Congress 1988d, 183).

Michael Hatch, commissioner of the Minnesota Department of Commerce, studied extensively the sales of long-term care insurance in his state during the mid-1980s. His findings reflect the nationwide pattern of fraud, intimidation, misrepresentation, and deception. For example, he found that "companies often induce seniors to purchase policies by emphasizing benefits which are seldom if ever available" (U.S. Congress 1988d, 58). He cites an example of a policy sold in Minnesota that guaranteed skilled nursing home benefits on the condition that the policyholder is in a nursing facility for at least 100 days and is in an "unstable health condition" during the entire duration of residency. The possibility that someone would remain in a nursing home with an unstable health condition for more than a few days is very unlikely.

"Few insureds ever meet the multitude of criteria necessary for obtaining skilled care or intermediate care benefits," according to Hatch (U.S. Congress 1988d, 58). He cites the not atypical example of an insurer who claims to provide care for Alzheimer's disease under the condition that the policyholder spend at least three days in a hospital to receive care for the specific condition that has led him or her to seek admission to a nursing home. The fact is, however, that very few Alzheimer's patients are hospitalized for that condition prior to being admitted to a nursing home. In other words, this policy would not cover most Alzheimer's patients for long-term care.

Many agents selling long-term care insurance to the elderly were found in the Minnesota study to use brutal and thoroughly unscrupulous tactics:

- Numerous agents selling long-term care insurance simply refused to leave the homes of seniors until they agreed to buy policies.
- One senior who balked at buying a policy reported that the agent threatened to return to her home in the future to watch as her assets were being auctioned off to pay for nursing home bills.
- Agents frequently used the opportunity once inside the home to sell seniors fraudulent shares in nonexistent investment programs.
- Some agents sold multiple worthless or unnecessary policies to seniors during the home visit. A number of cases were documented where the premiums generated by useless multiple policies exceeded 40 percent of the senior's gross annual income.

A study of insurance fraud and misrepresentation was recently released by Families USA Foundation, a private nonprofit foundation interested in the social well-being of senior citizens. Their research found that the most common problems included extensive delays in payments, outright denials to pay for legitimate claims, and misrepresentations by insurance agents. The study confirmed that many insurers sold policies by first exaggerating their coverage and then later refusing to pay promised benefits. The Families USA findings were corroborated by Rep. John Dingell (D-Mich.), who chairs the House Commerce Committee, which is engaged in similar investigations of the insurance industry. Families

USA Foundation has called for a full investigation of the situation by the Federal Trade Commission and has recommended as a solution to widespread insurance fraud and misrepresentation the establishment of a broad-based public-sector insurance program that would relegate the private insurance industry to a minor, supplementary role (Group Calls for Nursing Home Insurance Probe 1990). A GAO investigation of medigap sales abuses that was released in spring 1991 corroborates a number of the allegations made by Representative Dingell and the Foundation (Pullen 1991a).

Weak State Regulations

As noted in testimony during congressional hearings, Charles G. Brown, attorney general of West Virginia, said: "The present state regulatory framework consists of 50 different state systems offering largely ineffectual regulation by understaffed, underfunded, embattled state regulators who have consistently seen this economically and politically powerful industry lobby to erode and prevent significant or effective regulation (U.S. Congress 1988c, 14–15).

The National Association of Insurance Commissioners (NAIC) is a voluntary association composed of "the chief insurance regulatory officials of the fifty states, the District of Columbia and the four United States territories" (U.S. Congress 1988a, 11). NAIC provides a vehicle for the exchange of ideas among insurance commissioners and between insurance commissioners and insurance companies. In addition, the organization develops model insurance legislation and informational literature and reports and facilitates the collection of some types of data about the insurance industry.

The NAIC is a strictly voluntary organization. It has no enforcement powers whatsoever. Nevertheless, organization members spend a large part of their collective energies dealing with issues of fraud and corruption in the insurance industry. Because of the nationwide problem of targeting the elderly with health insurance fraud and deceptive marketing, one NAIC working group—the Medicare Supplement, Long-Term and Other Limited Benefit Plans Task Force (perhaps the most awkwardly named task force in the industry)—has recommended specific guidelines for insurance sold to consumers over sixty-five years of age. This association has initiated activity to deal with television advertising that is related to deceptive health insurance and with mass media lead cards that have been directed to senior citizens. For several years the NAIC has had in place a Long-Term Care Insurance Model Act formulated in part to counter fraudulent and deceptive versions of that type of insurance offered by the insurance industry. Finally, NAIC members founded in recent years a society of state market conduct examiners to train state department personnel to better keep track of widespread marketing misconduct among insurance firms (U.S. Congress 1988a). By mid-1991, however, the insurance industry had been shaken by several major failures fueled by corruption and fraud. NAIC appealed to the federal government to draft regulations to aid state regulators when pursuing interstate insurance crimes and criminals (Pullen 1991d).

Corruption of State Regulators

The insurance industry is nominally regulated by an insurance commissioner (or an equivalent designee) in every state. Throughout the United States about 6,500 employees work under insurance commissioners with a combined total budget approaching a third of a billion dollars (U.S. Congress 1988a, 12). An insurance commissioner who is an enthusiastic advocate on behalf of the state's consumers can save consumers tens or hundreds of millions of dollars in a given state and simultaneously limit insurance industry profits by an equal amount. Conversely, an insurance commissioner who is "responsive to the needs of the insurance industry" can be an extremely lucrative asset to the industry. As a result of the power of insurance commissioners to directly alter the profits of insurance companies, and as a result of the phenomenal sums of money involved, a significant number of insurance commissioners succumb to illegal industry temptation. In fact, so many succumb that in 1991 the Criminal Division of the Justice Department established a special insurance unit to investigate bribed commissioners as well as fraudulent insurers (Pullen 1991c). The following examples have been pulled primarily from a casual perusal of industry sources for an approximately eighteen-month period beginning January 1990.

Three Counts of Bribery

Gordon W. Taylor, Jr., was insurance commissioner of Wyoming until his sudden resignation at the end of 1989, shortly after two insurance companies under his jurisdiction went bankrupt. Within a few months the U.S. attorney for the District of Wyoming had charged Taylor with three counts of bribery. In the first count of bribery Taylor was charged with taking $8,250 from Roy E. Thigpen III, principal manager of Commercial General Insurance Company of Casper, Wyoming. Commercial General was one of the two companies that had gone belly up.

During an interview with special agents from the Wyoming attorney general's office, and in the presence of his personal attorney, Taylor recounted that late in 1988 he met Thigpen at a Cheyenne Holiday Inn. During this meeting Thigpen agreed to purchase thirty vacant lots owned by Taylor for $8,250 in cash and agreed in addition that no warranty deed would be recorded until the conclusion of Taylor's tenure as Wyoming insurance commissioner. The attorney general's office noted that they were "going to attempt to prove that as a result of the bribes, Mr. Taylor would have treated Mr. Thigpen's company more favorably than he would someone else" (Howard 1990, 46).

The second count of bribery involved the sale of Taylor's house to Robert Davis, owner of Lloyds, U.S., a Dallas-based insurance company. According to the attorney general's complaint, Davis had been attempting to move his insurance operations from Dallas to Wyoming. Davis bought the house from Taylor through an intermediary for $105,000 and sold it a few months later, incurring a net loss of approximately $37,000. The third charge of bribery involved representatives of the Laramie Insurance Company, according to the transcript of the interview with agents of the attorney general's office. Taylor had contacted these representatives to inquire if he could borrow their company jet to fly his family round-trip to Kansas City. In addition, Taylor borrowed a vehicle from one of the principal owners of the Laramie Insurance Company to drive his family on a pleasure jaunt to Arkansas (Former Wyoming Commissioner Indicted 1990). Former Wyoming insurance commissioner Gordon Taylor was sentenced to fifteen months in federal prison, fined $5,000, and required to perform 400 hours of community service (Ex-Wyoming Commissioner Sentenced 1991).

Commissioner Green Helps Out

In early summer 1990 the Louisiana House approved and sent to the governor legislation that would fine insurers who failed to pay a claim within thirty days $5,000 or twice the amount of the claim, whichever is greater. The sponsor of the bill was prompted to submit it as a result of the collapse of Champion Insurance Company, which left $150 million in unpaid claims. At about the same time, the state senate approved a bill that would allow Louisiana's attorney general to order an audit of an insurance firm if the company had not been audited by the Department of Insurance and a certified public accountant during the prior year. This legislation was opposed by Commissioner Doug Green but was approved on a 33–1 senate vote and sent to the House. While this flurry of legislative activity was taking place, Commissioner Green was facing federal charges of plotting with Champion Insurance Company to get elected so that he could help the financially shaky company survive (Bill Penalizing Insurers 1990).

Later in the summer of 1990 an East Baton Rouge Parish grand jury indicted insurance commissioner Doug Green, his wife, and his brother on charges of public bribery. According to a statement released by attorney general William Guste, in exchange for cash and services the commissioner agreed to influence the outcome of a state audit of Champion Insurance Company. The attorney general noted that the audit "concluded that Champion was solvent when in fact it was not" (Details of Champion Investigation Released 1990). In addition, the attorney general charged that Commissioner Green had been chosen by the owners of Champion Insurance Company as their candidate for insurance commissioner and that Champion had provided up to $3 million for Green's 1987 election campaign.

During that same summer of 1990 the U.S. Justice Department indicted Commissioner Green for money laundering, conspiracy, and sixteen counts of mail fraud in connection with bribe taking and misusing his position as insurance commissioner to benefit Champion (Justice Department Indicts 1990). The next summer the U.S. District Court sentenced Green to twenty-five years in prison. He could get an additional ten years for bribery charges, to which he has already pled guilty in state court (La. Commissioner Gets 25 Years 1991).

Additional cases uncovered during this eighteen-month period include the following:

- Former deputy insurance commissioner and now acting commissioner Hunter Wagner, who took the place of former commissioner Green (who was sentenced to jail), has agreed to absent himself from any regulatory actions involving Southshore Holding Co. or any of its insurance corporation affiliates. The Louisiana attorney general is currently conducting a criminal investigation of Southshore. Acting commissioner Wagner was a private consultant to Southshore during part of the period under investigation (Midwest Life Agrees to Supervision 1991).
- A scam involving the failed Victoria Insurance Co., Ltd., of Georgia left $20 million in unpaid bills. A special assistant to the Georgia attorney general investigating this case noted that James L. Bentley, Jr., former Georgia insurance commissioner, his son, James Bentley III, and Coy Johnson, former deputy insurance commissioner, were involved with setting up and/or operating Victoria (Pullen 1991d).
- R. W. Brayton worked at the Texas State Board of Insurance from 1976 to 1979. At that time he was in charge of the division that monitored and rehabilitated financially troubled companies. During the summer of 1990 he was indicted along with others on charges of theft and misapplication of funds in connection with his controlling interest in the failed First Southwest Lloyds Insurance Company of Austin, and his ownership of the insurance firm of R. W. Brayton & Co. (Texas Fraud Investigation 1990).
- Early in February 1991, Nevada insurance commissioner Al Iuppa was put on leave with administrative pay as a result of an investigation by a Nevada state assembly panel. He had been questioned in a meeting with the panel about failing to collect $7 million in insurance premium taxes and penalties

since 1989 and about his use of a state credit card. Weeks later, Iuppa resigned (Nev. Commissioner Put on Leave 1991; Nevada Commissioner Resigns 1991).

- James E. Long is the current North Carolina insurance commissioner and current president of the National Association of Insurance Commissioners. His former chief examiner, Bobby W. Gray, and an insurance company executive were charged in summer 1991 with "90 counts of bribery, mail and bank fraud, involving the alleged theft and misapplication, over five years, of more than $37 million in insurance premiums." (Knowles 1991a)

Taking from Medicare—Legally and Illegally

Some of the largest health insurance companies in the United States have been accused by federal investigators of misspending as much as $10 billion in Medicare funds during the past few years. The *Wall Street Journal* noted that this may be "the biggest financial scandal in the history of Medicare" (Pound and Bogdanich 1989). Perhaps more important, however, is that this is yet another example of illegal operations that appear to be considered "business as usual" among major corporate players in the health insurance industry.

There are approximately 1 million persons and their spouses in the United States who are over sixty-five years of age, continue to be employed, and consequently have private health insurance. These people are insured by both private health insurance plans and Medicare. In order to contain costs, in 1982 Congress mandated that Medicare is the "secondary insurer." This means that Medicare will pay only for claims not covered by private health insurance when a person is covered by both types of policies. The federal Health Care Financing Administration pays tens of millions of dollars each year to private subcontractors to monitor Medicare payments to make sure that as the secondary insurer Medicare is not paying benefits that are actually the responsibility of private insurers. Incredibly enough, most of the contractors are the very same private insurance companies that the government is attempting to monitor. Needless to say, this system has not worked very well.

A General Accounting Office (GAO) study, for example, determined that in 1985 Medicare paid at least $527 million for hospital claims that should have been paid largely by private health insurers. In another government study, a sample of Medicare payments totaling $112 million was investigated by the inspector general's office of the Department of Health and Human Services. Their study found that nearly $21 million, almost 19 percent of the total, should have been paid by other parties, mainly private health insurers. These costs, perhaps up to $10 billion in total, have been in effect transferred from private insurers to the elderly, in the form of higher deductibles and premiums for the Medicare insurance, and to the American taxpayer.

"What you have is a built-in incentive not to play ball with Medicare and a built-in conflict of interest," according to Frank Pasquier, who has been investigating Medicare programs for seven years for the General Accounting Office, as quoted in an article by the *Wall Street Journal* (Pound and Bogdanich 1989). Plenty of evidence of this conflict of interest has been found by a special task force composed of investigators from the inspector general's office of the Department of Health and Human Services, the Justice Department, and the U.S. Health Care Financing Administration. Some of their activities include investigations of major commercial health insurers such as Aetna Life and Casualty, Prudential Insurance Co. of America, Blue Cross/Blue Shield of Michigan, and Empire Blue Cross/Blue Shield in New York. In addition, a suit has been filed in federal court against Provident Life & Accident Insurance Co. alleging that it owes Medicare up to $223 million.

The government's case against Provident Life & Accident Insurance is particularly illuminating. According to documents filed in conjunction with the litigation, Provident employees were instructed to ignore cases in which Medicare was billed for health insurance claims that should have been paid by Provident. In a 1983 memo, a Provident associate regional manager wrote that "it is quite obvious to everyone that Medicare has no way of knowing who in their claim files is an active employee. Consequently, they never will be able to track this down and pass it back to the insurance industry" (Pound and Bogdanich 1989).

Documents involved with the Justice Department's case against Provident indicated that the insurance company maintained extensive records of the Medicare overpayments that involved its clients but that these records were destroyed. According to Provident's attorney, the records were no longer needed.

A recent follow-up study by the General Accounting Office, released in spring 1991, indicated that the problems outlined previously continue unabated. A major problem identified by the study involves the responsibility of the Health Care Financing Administration (HCFA) to assure that states use Medicaid to pay for a recipient's health care only after other health insurance resources have been used. "As a practical matter, HCFA's authority to enforce third-party requirements with financial penalties is almost nonexistent" (U.S. General Accounting Office 1991b, 1). HCFA's own studies found that forty-five of forty-nine states studied did not comply with at least one of the nine federal requirements that states must meet to assure the proper use of Medicaid funds. Over half the states studied did not comply with four or more requirements. An in-depth study of just California and Michigan indicated that backlogged claims for which private insurers may have some liability totaled in excess of $175 million.

Kickbacks

Raymond Maria is the director of the Office of Labor Racketeering, United States Department of Labor. He has "hard evidence" that a significant proportion of insurance agents and company representatives pay illegal kickbacks to corporate or union officials who select health and other benefit plans. Some government officials in the Departments of Labor and Justice go further: They believe that illegal kickbacks are widespread throughout the commercial insurance industry (Bradley and Hey 1988). As of late 1988 grand juries were convening in a number of the largest cities in the nation to investigate alleged illegal kickback activities by commercial insurance companies.

There are 4,400 benefit plans covering 120 million persons, but there are fewer than 300 Department of Labor investigators and auditors to monitor them. Fewer than 1 percent of these benefit plans are scrutinized by the Department of Labor in any given year. However, kickbacks can add up to 40 percent of the cost of a health insurance plan, and they are entirely illegal according to provisions in the federal racketeering law. According to Maria, these practices are not isolated just among insurance sales personnel but are known in the boardrooms at the higher levels of the insurance industry. "What we see emerging is a new generation of racketeers," Maria has been quoted as saying (Bradley and Hey 1988).

Multiple Employer Welfare Associations

Candor is so refreshing. The article in the insurance industry newsletter "Best's Insurance Management Reports" begins with an almost audible sigh of resignation: "The Senate has uncovered yet another fraudulent scheme in the insurance industry" (Pullen 1990f). Multiple employer welfare associations (MEWAs) and the similar multiple employer trusts (METs) in theory are insurance pools that small businesses join to reduce the cost of health insurance. Perhaps Senator Sam Nunn (D-Ga.) has best summed up what MEWAs frequently are in reality: "Many of these plans are being looted by unscrupulous operators, who use premium money to cover outrageous salaries and commissions, personal expenses and entertainment. . . . By the time anyone has caught on to this scheme, the operators usually have skipped town, often moving into another state in order to avoid the reach of state insurance authorities" (Pullen 1990f).

The Senate Permanent Subcommittee on Investigations heard a great deal of testimony about one such MEWA, Cap Staffing, Inc., of Charlotte,

North Carolina. According to reported testimony, Cap Staffing hired employees of member small businesses and leased them back with the understanding that Cap Staffing would take care of health benefits and other administrative functions. Cap Staffing management claimed that they could obtain a better rate for health insurance by grouping a number of small businesses under their wing. Moreover, Cap Staffing led insurance agents and small-business management to believe that the health insurance plan was fully covered by a policy with Travelers Insurance Company. It wasn't. Cap Staffing was in fact self-insured, and Travelers simply administered the policy. Travelers claims that they were also taken in by Cap Staffing to the tune of $864,000 worth of unreimbursed claims and that Cap Staffing fraudulently represented their relationship with Travelers to employers and employees. James E. Long, vice-president of the National Association of Insurance Commissioners and commissioner of insurance in North Carolina, testified that MEWAs are typically self-funded and carry no commercial insurance. As a result, they slip under both federal and state regulation. At the end of this chain of fraud and theft are a number of employees from businesses associated with Cap Staffing who have been left with sizeable unpaid medical bills (Pullen 1990f).

MEWAs were established in 1974 by the Employee Retirement Income Security Act (ERISA). This law exempted MEWAs from having to register with state insurance departments, from having to make deposits into state guarantee funds (which theoretically protect policyholders when insurance companies are declared insolvent), and from state regulation of almost every kind. A 1983 change in the federal law added a new layer of jurisdictional confusion by allowing states to regulate MEWAs but still not requiring the associations to notify the state that they were operating in it. States cannot regulate MEWAs if they don't know of their existence. Typically regulators find out about fraudulent or mismanaged MEWAs after the damage has been done and new victims created. Because MEWAs are exempt from participating in state guarantee funds, employee victims with unpaid medical bills have little recourse with the possible exception of a suit against employers or insurance agents (Robinson 1990). John Garamendi, the feisty insurance commissioner from California, has publicly advocated the complete elimination of MEWAs (Garamendi Outlines Health Insurance Reforms 1991).

Summary

Fraud, corruption, and misrepresentation are endemic to all levels of private health insurance. The National Association of Insurance Commissioners is incapable of effective nationwide self-regulation. State regulators are too weak and uncoordinated, too underfunded, or too corrupt to protect residents from being victimized by unscrupulous insurance companies and agents. As a group, the elderly are particularly vulnerable to victimization by unethical or fraudulent agents. In addition, small businesses are increasingly vulnerable to fraudulent or otherwise illegal health insurance scams.

chapter six

Price Fixing and Conspiracy

cartel . . . An association of industrialists, business firms, etc., for establishing a national or international monopoly by price fixing, ownership of controlling stock, etc.; trust.

—Webster's New World Dictionary, Second College Edition

The insurance industry as a whole has benefited perhaps more than any other industry from special legislation exempting it from state and federal controls. As a consequence of this special historical relationship between state regulation and the insurance enterprise, the industry has been able to eliminate or rigidly control intraindustry competition in some important respects. The commercial insurance industry is exempt from federal antimonopoly regulations. This legalizes conspiracies to fix prices, carve up territories, and standardize product offerings. Blue Cross/Blue Shield enjoys unique enabling legislation at both federal and state levels that gives each state or regional plan special exemptions from state regulation, relief from some local taxation, and an institutional monopoly in its respective territory. Federal legislation exempts self-funded health insurance plans from state regulation such as mandated benefits, minimum financial stability criteria, and other requirements that commercial insurers are supposed to adhere to for the benefit of consumers. All these legislated concessions to the insurance industry decrease certain types of competition among corporate players while adversely affecting consumers through the resulting higher costs, limited choices, inferior products, decreased protection against insurer insolvency, and greater difficulty in obtaining certain types of insurance. This chapter focuses on some of the more blatant abuses of the public trust by the commercial insurance industry.

Insurance Cartels

The first insurance cartel was established in the 1800s by fire insurers, who eventually became the modern property/casualty corporate monoliths of today. The purpose of the cartel was to protect high profit margins by sharing information, limiting and standardizing products, and fixing prices. The insurance industry was momentarily shakened in 1944 when the Supreme Court determined that the insurance business was subject to federal antitrust regulations. Within a year, however, in testimony to the political strength of the industry, the McCarran-Ferguson Act was passed, which exempted commercial insurers from federal antimonopoly regulation and left remaining regulation of the industry to individual states. The heart of the remaining insurance cartel was a nationwide network of eleven industry-controlled regional property and casualty rating bureaus that was essential to the price-fixing strategy of the industry. These rating bureaus were united in 1971 under one roof, Insurance Services Office (ISO). ISO established industrywide "advisory rates" that were high enough to generate profits typically in the range of 25 percent per year for many years (Welles and Farrell 1989; The State of California 1988). In 1980 the insurance industry further insulated itself from federal regulation by convincing Congress to prohibit the Federal Trade Commission from investigating insurance matters (Lipsen 1990).

As with any cartel, there are always centrifugal forces working to break up conspiratorial unity. In the case of the commercial property/casualty insurance industry, these have included price cutting by large insurers with armies of in-house sales agents, the attraction of domestic and international investors to high profits generated by the very success of the cartel itself, and the booming trend of self-insuring. Nevertheless, commercial insurers continue to dominate a large share of the market and do so with the help of a cartel-like national structure (Welles and Farrell 1989).

The Insurance Services Office

Today the Insurance Services Office represents about 1,400 commercial property/casualty insurers writing 95 percent of all casualty insurance nationwide. It provides a range of services for member companies including the development of standard policy forms, the filing of information with state regulators on behalf of member insurers, the collection of data about the profit and loss of various types of policies nationwide, the projection of future trends based on data analysis, and, until quite recently, the calculation of advisory rates for various lines of insurance (The State of California v. Hartford 1988). As a result of emerging nationwide political pressure to eliminate the insurance industry exemption from federal and state antimonopoly laws, in a "too little too late" response ISO has decided to stop issuing advisory rates. Instead, the office will issue "prospective loss costs," a major component of the former advisory rates that critics claim can be converted relatively easily into the equivalent of advisory rates. An ISO spokesperson is quoted as having said about this policy change, "It's been a long hard process. Critics call us a cartel" (Fisher 1989).

ISO provides various services for the following fifteen property/casualty lines of insurance (Insurance Services Office, Inc. 1987):

Personal Lines of Insurance

- Personal automobile
- Dwelling fire and allied lines
- Home owners' (including mobile home)
- Personal inland marine
- Personal insurance coverage (PIC), including personal liability and residence theft

Commercial Lines of Insurance

- Commercial automobile
- Boiler and machinery
- Commercial crime
- Farm
- General liability
- Commercial glass
- Commercial inland marine
- Commercial multiple line
- Nuclear energy liability
- Professional liability

ISO nominally provides no services for health insurance, life insurance, workers' compensation insurance, and a number of other types of insurance. Nevertheless, a detailed discussion of ISO specifically along with the more general issue of the insurance industry exemption from federal antimonopoly regulations is necessary in order to understand the health insurance sector of the industry:

- Federal exemption from antimonopoly regulations affecting the commercial insurance industry as a whole allows the life/health side of the industry to fix prices, carve up territories, standardize products, exchange information, and so on, just like the property/casualty side of the industry.

- Many of the larger companies that are members of ISO are multiline companies, or belong to groups of companies that operate in both sectors of industry: property/casualty and life/health.
- ISO influence over the cost, terms, and availability of certain types of insurance, such as medical malpractice insurance, does affect the cost and availability of health care, ultimately having an effect on the cost, availability, and practicality of health insurance.
- The myriad ways the insurance industry is able to stifle competition are much better documented on the property/casualty side than on the life/health side. An analysis of the property/casualty sector of the industry will assist in the determination of the extent to which similar processes may be operating in the life/health sector.

In addition, Clark Havighurst, longtime analyst of the insurance industry, suggested that in some respects the Health Insurance Association of America (HIAA) acts like the ISO for the commercial health insurers:

> The health insurance industry, through the Health Insurance Association of America (HIAA), engages in a great deal of mutual consultation on competitive strategies. Cost-containment measures—coverage of second opinions, for example—are regularly examined in HIAA forums, with individual insurers apparently disclosing rather than withholding the results of their experience. Moreover, insurers frequently tell the world and each other what the industry—as opposed to its individual members—is doing about the cost problem. Some years ago, when Dr. Paul M. Ellwood, Jr., proposed the concept of "Health Alliances"—mechanisms comparable to PPOs—the HIAA convened a committee to examine the proposal. I subsequently asked members of that committee if I could see the results of their discussions, but was told that, on advice of antitrust counsel, the report was not available. It is reasonable to wonder about the state of competition in an industry where the desirability of particular competitive initiatives was examined by industrywide committees. Just as the industry seemed to strive for consensus on what was legally too risky to undertake, there also appeared to be an attempt to reach general agreement on what was feasible in cost containment. (Havighurst 1988, 243–244)

Nineteen States Sue Insurers for Antitrust Violations

Eight state attorneys general filed suit on March 23, 1988, charging federal and state antitrust violations among ISO, a number of insurers and reinsurers (organizations that back up insurance for insurers), brokers, and other parties in and out of the United States. Prior to taking this drastic action the states coordinated a two-year investigation that involved interviews and depositions of hundreds of witnesses and the accumulation of over 100,000 pages of documentary evidence (U.S.

Congress 1988c, 4). Ten additional states entered the suit within a short period of time. Although state laws differ, under the terms of the 1946 federal McCarran-Ferguson legislation insurers are in effect a legalized monopoly. They may meet and fix prices, standardize policies, and exchange other crucial information to reduce competition among themselves. As a result, insurers may appear to be competitive in the arena of sales and services, but they are not competitive in the arena of prices and policies. However, the McCarran-Ferguson legislation specifically prohibits the use of intimidation, boycott, and coercion by insurers in order to reduce competition. The suit by eighteen attorneys general was based on the allegation of the use of some or all of these prohibited activities by defendants. The suit itself is quite complex and does not deal specifically with health insurance. However, some of the allegations are extremely interesting in terms of shedding light on the operation of the insurance industry as a whole as well as suggesting potential consequences for the health insurance segment of the industry.

The original antitrust lawsuit brought by nineteen attorneys general against the insurance industry was dismissed in 1989 by federal district judge William Schwarzer. This dismissal did not come as a surprise to those who knew the judge. His record indicated that he had ruled for defendants or dismissed claims in over 90 percent of the cases that had come before him involving allegations of antitrust violations (Labaton 1988). Curiously, the judge argued that the actions of the defendants in the nineteen suits were immune from prosecution under the McCarran-Ferguson Act. This ruling was made despite the fact that the states alleged that the defendants were involved in intimidation, boycotts, and coercion—all of which are specifically prohibited under the McCarran-Ferguson Act.

The Justice Department and thirteen states subsequently filed friend-of-the-court briefs in a federal circuit court in San Francisco urging reversal of Judge Schwarzer's seemingly inappropriate dismissal of the lawsuit (Justice Dept. Backs States 1990). During spring 1991 a three-judge panel of the U.S. Court of Appeals for the Ninth Circuit overturned Judge Schwarzer's decision. In a unanimous decision, the panel of judges determined that a boycott had been organized and that the insurers had relinquished their antitrust exemption because they coordinated with unregulated foreign companies not covered by the exemption (Appellate Court Revives Antitrust Suit 1991).

Only a Few Insurers Control ISO

Despite the fact that ISO has about 1,400 corporate members, control of the organization seems to be highly concentrated among relatively few of those members. And, according to the suit filed by the State of

Texas against ISO and other defendants, those who control ISO are in a key position to squelch competition in the industry. The Texas suit is a bit different—perhaps a bit more revealing about industry practices than the others because the Texas suit was brought under more restrictive Texas regulations rather than under the federal antitrust laws:

> Defendant ISO is operated through an Executive Committee taken from the Board of Directors, and various other committees appointed by the membership or by the Board of Directors. Under the ISO Articles of Incorporation and Bylaws, ISO committees are composed of individuals. In reality, however, insurance companies act as the members of the committees. Some companies rotate employees as the company's "representative" on a committee. Further, individual companies often present their company's position on an issue through their corporate representative. Thus, in actuality, the board rooms and committee rooms of Defendant ISO are the forums for agreements in restraint of trade in violation of the Antitrust Act of the State of Texas.
>
> From the beginning of 1982 until the end of 1986, only 37 different companies, comprising approximately 2.8 percent of the ISO membership, served on the ISO Board of Directors. Further, 8 to 12 large primary companies, including the primary insurer Defendants, consistently controlled the Executive Committee. The primary insurer Defendants, comprising approximately 0.6 percent of the membership of ISO, dominated the ISO committee structure and thereby controlled ISO. (The State of Texas v. Insurance 1988)

Another interesting allegation in the Texas suit involves insurer agreements and actions in violation of Texas antitrust laws with intent to influence legislation:

> Plaintiff further alleges that Defendants herein entered into agreements in violation of the Antitrust Act to artificially constrict industry-wide capacity to provide general liability insurance, to thereby raise and stabilize prices, and to boycott particular lines, providers, and consumers of insurance, in order to create the necessary crisis atmosphere to promote tort reform and policy reform.

A number of industry leaders are cited in the Texas suit as advocating various aspects of the strategy outlined earlier. Among the most interesting of the aspects is the following:

> On June 18th, the *Journal of Commerce* reported that, shortly before becoming the chief executive officer for Defendant Fireman's Fund, John J. Byrne told a meeting of the Casualty Actuaries of New York: "It is right for the industry to withdraw and let the pressures for reform build in the

> courts and in the state legislatures. . . . The sooner the industry quits such lines of business, the sooner it will free itself from a court system that has run amok." Mr. Byrne was also quoted on June 24, 1985, in *Best's Insurance Management Reports:* ". . . withdrawing from certain lines such as product liability . . . will eventually bring home the message to state and federal lawmakers." (The State of Texas v. Insurance 1988, 34)

The State of Texas settled with ISO and a number of insurers for a figure of several million dollars. None admitted to breaking the law.

Insurers Boycott West Virginia

In the state of West Virginia in 1986, for example, according to the then attorney general, commercial medical malpractice insurers boycotted the state, refusing to sell that type of insurance in West Virginia because the insurers did not like existing tort laws in the state.

> I filed an antitrust case, submitted testimony that we would see our clinics shut down, our ambulances services, our kidney dialysis units, our doctors and baby doctors in rural areas and so on—basically an absolute catastrophe to the State of West Virginia—an insurance industry decision that they would put a gun to our head in order to get the tort reform that they wanted. With the injunction that I got, the industry was deprived of that weapon, an illegal weapon if you will, of using concerted economic action to reach a certain political end. (U.S. Congress 1988c, 3)

In a related case in New Jersey, the appellate division of the superior court in June 1991 upheld a state law requiring insurers who boycott auto insurance sales in the state to surrender their licenses to sell all other lines of insurance (N.J. Appeals Court Upholds 1991). In addition, a number of other states have successfully accomplished, or are vigorously pursuing, legislation to end or curtail insurance industry antimonopoly exemptions locally and nationally. Perhaps the most telling evidence of popular sentiment in this regard was from a Texas referendum held in March 1990 on whether the insurance industry should be allowed to fix prices. Nine of every ten voters said no (Lipsen 1990).

During the 1990 annual meeting of the American Bar Association, a special session was devoted to the effect of recent developments in federal and state antitrust legislation on life and health insurers. That this special session took place is interesting in itself because of the lack of publicly available documentation concerning the extent to which the life/health side of the industry legally conspires to minimize operation of the free market. In any case, Thomas Workman, partner in the law firm of Bricker and Eckler in Ohio, warned that life and health insurers could expect plenty of litigation from ongoing developments in this area. He noted that the precedent-setting 1988 vote in California known as Proposition 3 directed state antimonopoly legislation against the insurance industry but allowed the continuing exchange of selected types of information among insurers. In 1990 seven other states were considering antimonopoly legislation similar to California's. Three states were considering resolutions requesting that Congress repeal the McCarran-Ferguson Act, and three additional states were considering legislation that would apply state antimonopoly regulations to the insurance industry with no special exceptions (Arndt 1990a).

Insurance Lobby Fights for McCarran-Ferguson

Federal legislation to abolish or modify McCarran-Ferguson has been floated in recent years, invariably faced with massive lobbying activity by the insurance industry attempting to block it. In 1988 the House Judiciary Committee Subcommittee on Economic and Commercial Law approved a bill limiting the insurance industry exemption from antimonopoly regulation. Intense insurance industry lobbying killed the bill before it reached the House floor. A similar bill, H.R. 1663, sponsored by judiciary committee chairman Jack Brooks (D-Tex.), passed out of the subcommittee in summer 1990 by a partisan 9–6 vote and then passed out of the full judiciary committee by a 19–17 vote. This legislation would have modified McCarran-Ferguson by allowing insurers to share information about claims filed but would have barred the insurance industry from current practices including price fixing, carving up and allocating sales territories among "competitors," and bundling unrelated products with insurance policies. Furthermore, offending insurers could be sued by state attorneys general, the Justice Department, the Federal Trade Commission, private individuals, and corporations. Senator Howard Metzenbaum (D-Ohio) introduced similar legislation in the Senate (Pullen 1990a; Committee Passes Bill 1990; House Subcommittee Passes Bill 1990).

In a blatant example of insurance industry political muscle, nine members of Congress who were former insurance agents sent a joint letter to every member of the House excoriating H.R. 1663 and urging their colleagues not to vote for it. This group was not a collection of congressional lightweights. Notable among them were Jerry Lewis (R-Calif.), chairman of the House Republican Conference; James H. Quillen (R-Tenn.), ranking minority member of the House Rules Committee; and Butler Derrick (D-S.C.) and Gerald B. Solomon (R-N.Y.), both senior members of the House Rules Committee (Fisher 1990).

In an additional lobbying thrust, the National Association of Life Underwriters (NALU) sent an alert to its total membership of 140,000 urging political action to keep Representative Brooks's H.R. 1663 off the floor of the House. The American Council of Life Insurance (ACLI) sent a mailing to 40,000 individuals that urged them to contact their representatives to kill H.R. 1663. This action was part of one of the council's largest lobbying efforts to date. The goal of these activities is to send the House of Representatives "a blizzard of letters and phone calls from industry professionals seeking to protect the McCarran-Ferguson Act" (Brostoff 1990a). Although positions of specific organizations sometimes change rather rapidly, the industry as a whole appears to be split on the McCarran strategy. Some segments are fighting to protect the McCarran legislation at any cost, and others advocate fronting alternative legislation designed to protect major interests of the insurance industry while removing the political heat (Some Insurers Concede 1991).

Summary

The commercial insurance industry grew and prospered during this century in large part because it was organized as a legal cartel. The path to legal conspiracy was further cleared in midcentury by McCarran-Ferguson. The Blues also have had special regional monopolies granted by federal and state laws. Although the documented evidence is more complete for cartel-like behavior among the property/casualty insurers rather than life/health insurers, there are enough relationships between the two types of insurers to warrant questions regarding similar collusion among health insurers. Widespread social impact of coordinated insurance industry boycotts, industrywide massive price increases, and standardization of inferior products have led to a growing challenge of the insurance industry's exemption from federal antimonopoly regulations.

chapter seven

Insolvencies: Insurance Companies That Cannot Pay Claims

As the subcommittee's inquiry has progressed, we have observed a remarkable record of greed and incompetence by the persons responsible for managing these companies. The records include excessive underpricing, ridiculous underwriting, illusory reinsurance, reckless management, self-dealing, non-existent records, and a general concern only for the welfare of the top corporate insiders. These acts have been masked by contrived transactions, creative accounting and fraudulent reports to regulatory agencies.

—Rep. John D. Dingell, Chair, House Subcommittee on Oversight and Investigations, hearings on insurance company failures

The Magnitude of the Insolvency Crisis

Early in 1990 an internal report analyzing the life/health insurance industry was completed by IDS Financial Services, a unit of American Express (Laing 1990). The report reached startling conclusions about the near future of the insurance industry. The IDS study predicted, for example, that up to one-third of the 100 largest life/health insurance companies will probably collapse during the 1990s. This catastrophic event would simply cap the rising trend of insurance company failures during the past twenty years. During the 1970s an average of five life/health insurers per year were declared insolvent. In 1988 alone ten life/health insurers were declared insolvent, and in the first seven months of 1990 a record twenty-nine went belly up. A major portion of the insurance sold by these insolvent companies was centered in the health and accident lines of insurance (Life/Health Corporate Changes 1990). During 1988 and 1989 an annual average of $77 million was assessed the insurance industry by state guarantee funds to cover the losses of their insolvent corporate kin. This figure is sixty-four times larger than the comparable figure in the peak recession year of 1975.

Property and casualty insurance companies that failed in the late 1960s and 1970s were usually smaller companies that sold automobile insurance in a state or limited region. The situation changed radically in the 1980s because companies were larger and more complex. The reasons for failure included "underpricing premiums, underreserving for losses, problems with risk-sharing arrangements, fraud or incompetence, and overexpansion" (U.S. Congress 1989a, 601). From the 1970s to the 1980s the average annual number of property/casualty insurance company liquidations doubled from six to twelve. The number of companies considered financially shaky by the National Association of Insurance Commissioners quadrupled from 132 in 1979 to 569 in 1988. The latter figure represents over 20 percent of the insurance companies reviewed that year. These companies are a ticking time bomb for the industry and for the policyholders.

Analysts often treat property and casualty (P/C) insurers separately from life and health (L/H) insurers in discussions of insolvency. There is some justification for this because a couple of the specific causes of insolvency differ for the two types of companies. However, from the perspective of an industrywide crisis the distinction breaks down for several reasons.

Many of the larger insurance companies are multiline companies. This means that they have P/C divisions that sell primarily property and casualty insurance and L/H divisions that sell primarily life and health lines of insurance. Serious financial difficulties on one side of the company obviously affect the other side of the company. Even insurance companies that are considered to be strictly property and casualty insurers often sell health insurance, selling a few percent of all commercial health insurance sold in the United States. Insolvencies in these companies will affect those who have health insurance policies with them. Both P/C and L/H insurers are also frequently linked in terms of sharing liability for insurance company insolvencies through state guarantee funds, as discussed later.

Similarities to the Savings and Loan Failures

Rep. John D. Dingell of Michigan is chair of the Subcommittee on Oversight and Investigations of the House Committee on Energy and Commerce. For several years his subcommittee has embodied the principal federal effort investigating the increasingly serious problem of insurance company failures across the United States, although recently a parallel investigation by the Treasury Department has been initiated (Brostoff 1991c). In the opening remarks of his 1990 summary report on the matter, Representative Dingell made these frightening and unequivocal observations:

> The parallels between the present situation in the insurance industry and the early states of the savings and loan debacle are both obvious and deeply disturbing. They encompass scandalous mismanagement and rascality by certain persons entrusted with operating insurance companies, along with an appalling lack of regulatory controls to detect, prevent, and punish such activities. Because the ill effects of fraud and gross incompetence may be hidden for 10 years or more after a policy is written, the problems observed by the Subcommittee could quickly escalate into a real threat to the solvency of the insurance industry if reforms are not implemented very soon. (U.S. Congress 1990a, III)

Representative Dingell's understanding of the similarities between the savings and loan disaster and the escalating problem of insurance industry failures came in large part from the testimony of Frederick D. Wolf (U.S. Congress 1989a). Wolf is the assistant comptroller general of the Accounting and Financial Management Division of the General Accounting Office. His expertise is unparalleled in terms of understanding the relationships between these two financial industries because he has conducted in-depth comprehensive studies of both. During the period September 1987 through March 1989, Wolf intensively reviewed twenty-six thrifts that had failed during the twenty-one months that preceded September 1987. Concurrently, Wolf analyzed the failures of two large property/casualty insurance companies and reviewed a variety of documents relating to the insurance industry as a whole. Although some elements of his findings refer specifically to the property/casualty side of the insurance industry, most of his findings are equally applicable to the life/health side of the industry as well. As a result of his investigations, he found the following similarities in the characteristics of both failed savings and loans and failed insurance companies:

1. Multiple regulators
2. Growth orientation and expansion of markets
3. Excessive underpricing and minimal or poor underwriting
4. Imprudent management practices
5. Extensive and complex reinsurance (comparable to loan participations at thrifts)
6. Long lapses between examinations
7. Inadequate internal controls

8. Inadequate loss reserves
9. Change from traditional to potentially riskier activities
10. Outdated audit guide

In addition to these similarities, Wolf compared and contrasted state guaranty funds and the Federal Savings and Loan Insurance Corporation (FSLIC) deposit insurance. In the case of insurance insolvencies Wolf also found that extensive use of managing general agents contributed to financial difficulties, although there is no comparable element in the savings and loan industry. In any case, these similarities are so striking and so pervasive that it is worthwhile to look at each separately as they apply to the insurance industry.

Multiple Regulators

Wolf noted that the savings and loan industry is regulated by both federal and state regulations, depending on the origin of the institution's charter and whether its deposits are insured by the federal government. Frequently, state-chartered savings and loan institutions were allowed "to engage in riskier activities than those permitted by the federal regulator" and these practices often resulted in large losses, which contributed to the failures of many savings and loans. He pointed out that in the case of the insurance industry there is only the multiplicity of state regulation, so the problem of adequate standardized regulation is even more pronounced (U.S. Congress 1989a, 612). Representative Dingell has focused a great deal of blame on the chaos of state regulation:

> Enforcement of insurance laws and regulations is one of the weakest links in the present regulatory system. States apparently are not collecting adequate information, investigating wrongdoing, or taking legal action against the perpetrators of insolvency. Statutory penalties and remedies also seem out-of-step with the realities of today's insurance market. With little fear of meaningful administrative sanctions or criminal prosecution, there is no effective penalty for wrongdoing and no real deterrent. Inadequate enforcement was a major factor in the scandals and gross incompetence that accompanied the collapse of the savings and loan industry. (U.S. Congress 1990a, 74)

Again, in the characteristically blunt but colorful words of Representative Dingell: "The regulatory system must anticipate and deal effectively with the activities of the pirates and dolts who inevitably will plague an attractive industry such as insurance, where customers hand over large sums of cash in return for a promise of future benefits" (U.S. Congress 1990a, III).

The insurance industry and state regulators typically claim that more effective state regulation of the insurance industry can be developed by a long-standing voluntary organization, the National Association of Insurance Commissioners (NAIC). A recently released GAO assessment of the NAIC cast serious doubt that neither NAIC nor the states can ever effectively regulate insolvencies or other major aspects of the insurance industry. In his summary statement to the Subcommittee on Oversight and Investigations of the House Committee on Energy and Commerce, Richard L. Fogel, assistant comptroller general, made these observations:

> Although insurance is a national market, the state-by-state system of insurance solvency regulation is characterized by varying regulatory capacities and a lack of uniformity. . . .
>
> NAIC is trying to establish a national system of effective solvency regulation through its accreditation program. In effect, NAIC has assumed the role of a regulator of state insurance regulators. However, we do not believe that state adoption of NAIC's current standards will achieve a consistent and effective system of solvency regulation. The underlying standards for accreditation are often undemanding and, in some cases, inadequate.
>
> Even if NAIC devised sufficiently stringent standards for effective solvency regulation, however, we do not believe that NAIC can surmount the fundamental barriers to its long-term effectiveness as a regulator. Most importantly, NAIC lacks authority to enforce its standards. . . .
>
> NAIC does not have the authority necessary to compel state action or to sustain its reforms. We do not believe it can effectively be given such authority, at least on a lasting basis, by either the states or the federal government. The main road to effective regulation of the insurance industry does not pass through NAIC. (Fogel 1991, 32–33)

Joseph Belth is professor of insurance at Indiana University and editor of the watchdog *Insurance Forum.* He has frequently argued that life/health insurers often ignore the statutory accounting principles (SAP), the industry accounting standard supported by the NAIC. This subterfuge ultimately results in surpluses appearing larger than they actually are and companies appearing solvent when they actually are not. The biggest problem, according to Belth, is that a significant number of state insurance regulators knowingly let the insurance companies perpetrate these accounting scams.

He discussed the example of Life Assurance of Pennsylvania, which filed a 1989 annual statement that indicated a statutory surplus of approximately $8 million. The surplus was based on a reinsurance transaction with American Standard Life and Accident, for which Life Assurance claimed $8 million credit. There was, however, one little problem. American Standard was in conservatorship in a dispute about the value of the firm's holdings. The California insurance department issued a cease-and-desist order based on their belief that the company was insolvent by $32 million. However, the insurance department in Pennsylvania, where Life Assurance is headquartered, found nothing wrong with the reinsurance deal, and Life Assurance continued to operate as usual in that state (Fenske 1990).

Growth Orientation and Expansion of Markets

Wolf found that failed savings and loan institutions typically pursued "excessively growth-oriented strategies." These strategies

> resulted from management decisions to attempt to generate increased earnings which resulted in compromising the safety and soundness of the institutions' credit and investment policies. These strategies were implemented by soliciting deposits at above market rates and using the proceeds to make loans and investments of a highly speculative nature, often of dubious economic value. While this resulted in rapid growth, such growth was accompanied by increased—and often fatal—risk. (U.S. Congress 1989a, 604)

The two insurance companies studied by Wolf also experienced rapid growth. Between 1979 and 1984 one company experienced a 63 percent increase of premiums and the other company a 182 percent increase.

Excessive Underpricing and Minimal or Poor Underwriting

The rapid growth of the failed insurers was accomplished in large part by a policy advocating the extreme underpricing of the policies being sold. This underpricing captured a lot of business in the market in the short run, but the premiums and investment incomes generated by the insurance companies could not cover the claims and expenses that the companies needed to pay over time. This type of growth strategy is called "cash flow underwriting."

Extensive Use of Managing General Agents

The use of managing general agents (MGAs) in the insurance industry is fairly extensive. In this practice, insurance companies contract with independent agents, MGAs, to conduct a wide range of insurance business in the company's name. This fosters the rapid growth of the company while minimizing overhead. The MGAs are paid on the basis of commissions they receive tied to how much insurance they sell. The failed insurance companies made excessive use of MGAs, were not able to control or monitor the business that MGAs conducted in the name of the company, and were ultimately financially responsible for risky and careless profit-maximizing behavior of the contracted MGAs.

Imprudent Management Practices

Various aspects of this topic are discussed in other sections in this chapter. However, Representative Dingell, in his inimicable manner, unhesitatingly pointed his finger at a singularly important cause of imprudent management practices:

> The business of insurance is uniquely suited to abuse by mismanagement and fraud. Making believable promises is a stock item in every con man's bag of tricks. The prepayment of large, often vast, sums of money with few restrictions lends itself naturally to monumental wasting of assets through greed, incompetence, and dereliction of duty. This combination of easy money based on easy promises makes the insurance industry an irresistible target for financial knaves and buccaneers. (U.S. Congress 1990a, 3)

Extensive and Complex Reinsurance

Reinsurance involves the purchase of an additional layer of insurance by one insurance company from another. For a fee, the reinsurer agrees to cover all or some of the claims made upon the company that purchased the reinsurance. Reinsurance purchased by the failed insurers or their MGAs was frequently purchased from companies that were themselves financially marginal or insolvent. Other reinsurers simply refused to pay claims that they felt were the result of poor underwriting, that is, the result of unnecessarily risky policies written by the insurer or their MGAs. The refusal or inability of reinsurers to pay claims added to the mountain of debts that drove the insurance companies into insolvency. According to Myron M. Picoult, analyst for Oppenheimer and Co., as much as $16 billion worth of reinsurance may be illusory and uncollectible (Welles and Farrell 1989). Reinsurance rates, contracts, and offshore reinsurers are almost entirely unregulated at any level. Frederick Wolf of the GAO observed that "the problems experienced with reinsurance agreements are similar to those we have noted with reverse repurchase agreements and loan participations in the securities, banking, and thrift industries" (U.S. Congress 1989a, 610).

Long Lapses Between Examinations

A recent survey of forty-seven state insurance departments by the National Association of Professional Insurance Agents and the Consumer Insurance Interest Group found that fewer than half of the insurance departments that responded conduct financial examinations of insurance companies headquartered in their state at least once every three years. The study also found that in most states regulators lack the resources to effectively monitor insurance companies for solvency. They discovered, moreover, that 40 percent of the state insurance departments cannot retrieve statistical data on previous financial examinations (U.S. Congress 1989a, 613).

Wolf and other GAO investigators found that failed savings and loan institutions that were examined as often as once a year did not provide sufficient time for regulators to act. The failed insurance companies they analyzed were examined every three years.

Inadequate Internal Controls

Every failed savings and loan examined by the GAO had serious financial and business record shortcomings. Among the most frequently noted were documentation deficiencies and the understatement of loss reserves, that is, reserve funds set aside to make up for bad loans or faltering real estate. The two analyzed insurance companies also shared these same problems. One of the failed insurers, for example, lacked records indicating who all their reinsurers were. The other had no central record of insurance policies written or premiums due or collected.

A related problem involves the way insurance companies do their internal accounting and how they report the results to regulators. States can allow or mandate different accounting procedures among insurers with a variety of consequences. The nominal insurance industry accounting procedures standard, statutory accounting practices (SAP), can result in an overstatement of net worth compared with standard accounting practices used by other types of businesses. This overstatement can distort important information needed by the regulators. As a result of these and other reasons, Wolf stated quite unequivocally that "it cannot be expected that the annual financial information reported to state regulators, or to NAIC [National Association of Insurance Commissioners] will be accurate or reliable" (U.S. Congress 1989a, 623).

Inadequate Loss Reserves

Of twenty-six failed thrifts examined by the GAO, eighteen had insufficient loss reserves to cover anticipated losses from declining real estate and uncollectible loans. Insurers also require reserves to cover claims filed but not paid and claims incurred but not yet reported. Neither of the investigated failed insurance companies had adequate reserves. In fact, neither of them employed actuaries (insurance industry mathematicians) to accurately estimate risks so that the reserves could also be accurately estimated. The problem of inadequate reserves is an industrywide problem. According to Brookings Institute economist Robert E. Litan, the Insurance Services Office estimated that by the end of 1988 loss adjustment expenses reserves, which made up about 30 percent of all property/casualty losses, were at least 50 percent deficient. This deficiency, combined with deficiencies in other types of industry loss reserves, indicates that many insurers currently suspected of being financially unstable are already insolvent (Pullen 1990e).

Change from Traditional to Potentially Riskier Activities

The GAO investigation found that "virtually all of the failed thrifts in our review expanded from traditional home mortgage lending to lending and investment in high-risk activities" (U.S. Congress 1989a, 606). The pattern was much the same with the failed property/casualty insurers. They expanded from traditional areas of insurance into high-risk commercial liability areas such as chemical companies, toxic waste, and others.

A different but comparable phenomenon occurred with the life/health side of the insurance industry. During the 1970s and early 1980s the life insurance line of life/health insurers began to see fierce competition in the area of consumer savings from other financial institutions such as the savings and loan industry. As a result, life insurers expanded into a variety of high-yield products like fixed-income pension offerings such as guaranteed investment contracts (GICs) and universal life. Depending on the product, investment options were expanded to include money markets and stock and bond mutual funds. The end result of this confusing outpouring of financial products was that the entire investment risk, including both principal and interest, accumulated with the insurers. Because of this process, their exposure to loss has risen dramatically over the past couple of decades. In addition, the relatively new high-yield products have sometimes cut deeply into profitability, further weakening the industry.

Summing up a few of the critical historical forces contributing to the growing financial instability of life/health insurers, Jonathan Laing, business reporter for *Barron's,* has written: "No longer are insurers mere providers of protection against death, disability and illness. Today, they are both quasi depositories and daredevils, forced to push their investments into the outer envelope of yield in order to deliver lush guaranteed returns on their life, annuity and CD-like GICs—and still make a profit" (Laing 1990).

Outdated Audit Guide

The industry guide for auditing savings and loan institutions had not been substantially revised since 1979 despite massive changes in the industry. Standards for auditing the insurance industry were established previously by the American Institute of Certified Public Accountants in 1966. These standards were slightly amended in 1982, and only in the late 1980s have they been undergoing a complete rewriting and public review process. In both cases, adequate directions for locking the barn door in time were nowhere to be found.

Additional Causes of Insolvencies

Shaky as many of these companies look on paper, they are in fact even shakier: "A number of companies have managed to inflate their surpluses artificially by manipulating policy reserves, using sales and leasebacks of offices and equipment to affiliated companies, entering into dubious reinsurance schemes and employing 'levelized' commission programs to disguise heavy first-year pay-outs to insurance agents" (Laing 1990, 10).

Add to this the declining quality of the life/health insurers' general accounts assets. These funds are the foundation of the insurers' policies and guaranteed products. The insurance industry owns $60 billion worth of junk bonds, that is, highly risky below-investment-grade corporate IOUs. This is one-third of all outstanding junk bonds in existence and four times the amount of junk held by the savings and loan industry (Thompson 1990). A total of $20 billion worth of junk bonds defaulted in 1990. This amount is double that of defaults the previous year and four times more than the year before that (Berner and Rahl 1991). These bonds account for about 6.4 percent of total invested assets in the life/health insurance industry, which doesn't sound like much until it is compared with total industry capital, which equals approximately 6.5 percent of assets. Put in another way: "So, the industry has nearly the equivalent of virtually its entire net worth riding on an illiquid investment sector that has been in a free fall for the past year and threatens to get a lot worse" (Laing 1990, 11).

For some life/health insurers, data reflecting aggregate industrywide holdings of junk bonds obscure a far more desperate situation. A recent study by the National Association of Insurance Commissioners found that eighteen life/health insurers held more than 30 percent of their assets in junk bonds. Three of the largest holders of junk bonds are subsidiaries of Executive Life Insurance Company, which had a total of $6.4 billion in junk bonds out of $10.1 billion in total assets. Executive Life and all its subsidiaries have been seized by state regulators and are not allowed to write any new policies pending the outcome of severe financial problems (Maxey 1991). The seizure is the largest regulatory takeover ever of a commercial life/health insurance company and certainly will not be the last. Martin Weiss (no relation to the author), of Weiss Research, rates the financial standing of about 1,700 life/health insurance companies. In spring 1991 he determined that well over a third of them, including some of the biggest, would probably fail in the event of a severe recession (Kristof 1991).

Bad News in Real Estate Holdings

There is more discomforting news in the real estate holdings of the life/health insurance industry. The panic sales of foreclosed savings and loan and bank properties are driving down the value of the insurance industry's current commercial real estate mortgages and direct investments, which amount to 24 percent of general accounts holdings. This devaluation took place along with declining real estate values resulting from the rolling recession of the past few years. Delinquencies among insurer-held commercial mortgages have tripled in the past decade. Some 40 percent of the life insurance industry's directly held properties (which represent about one-tenth of total real estate assets) have already been foreclosed. Among the top ten insurers suffering from mortgage delinquencies and foreclosures (in process or completed) are some of the biggies such as Aetna, UNUM, Travelers, Mutual Benefit, John Hancock Mutual, and Equitable. The top twenty-five life/health insurance companies are expected to lose $3.3 billion as a result of souring real estate assets over the next three years. The stocks of many of these insurers and others in the past year have dropped 40 percent or more (Laing 1990; Crosson 1991a). This situation is not the picture of an industry at the apex of financial stability.

In summer 1991 Moody's Investors Service, Inc., a major insurance industry rating service, lowered the rating of six major insurance companies in terms of their ability to pay claims. These companies included Travelers Insurance Co., John Hancock Mutual Life Insurance Co., Massachusetts Mutual Life Insurance Co., Mutual Life Insurance Co. of New York, New England Mutual Life Insurance Co., and Principal Mutual Life Insurance Co. In large part the reduced ratings resulted from the declining value of real estate holdings (Crenshaw 1991). A few months later Moody's announced that it intended to lower the ratings of several more life insurance companies because of more timely regulatory actions and declining public confidence in the insurance industry. This is the so-called run risk factor—the possibility of policyholders withdrawing large amounts of cash in a short period of time because they fear insurer financial instability. At about the same time, Standard & Poor's Corp., another major insurance industry rating service, announced that during 1991 it had downgraded the financial health rating of twenty-three insurers and upgraded only one. In addition, it noted that of the 2,600 companies it reviewed, over 500 appeared financially vulnerable. Approximately 13 percent of the $457 billion of insurance premiums their review covered was placed with companies rated only adequate or vulnerable (Caprino 1991; Insurers' Ratings May Slip 1991).

Finally, a couple of recent studies indicated that rapid rises or falls in interest rates could contribute to insolvencies in a number of life/health insurers (Berg 1990). A report by the New York investment advisory firm of Eastbridge Capital, Inc., noted that larger life insurance companies sell popular guaranteed investment contracts (GICs), which guarantee the purchaser a certain return on the invested premium of the policy. If interest rates fall sharply, the insurer will not be able to earn as much on its investments as it is obligated to pay on the GIC. Small and medium-sized life insurance companies, however, may find themselves in deep financial trouble if interest rates rise dramatically. Many of these companies sell a type of life insurance policy that allows the purchaser to borrow against it at a relatively low fixed rate of interest. If interest rates rise significantly, there may be a surge of borrowing this cheap money by policyholders. Marginal insurers would then be forced to borrow at considerably higher rates to remain liquid. Another recent study by a subsidiary of American Express Co. has reached similar conclusions. Both studies questioned the level of preparedness and the financial ability of life/health insurers to weather these possible economic storms.

There are indications that the situation is getting worse—much worse—rather than better. A freshly released study by the Townsend & Schupp Company, an investment banking and credit research firm specializing in the insurance industry, analyzed the ratio of high-risk assets to total surplus (i.e., assets minus liabilities). They looked at 101 companies with 71 percent of the total assets of the life insurance industry. In 1989 the high-risk assets to total surplus ratio was 91 percent. By the end of 1990 it had soared to 140 percent. Eight of these leading life insurers had high-risk assets, mostly junk bonds, surpassing 500 percent of total surplus. During the first half of 1991 four of these eight companies have been taken over by state insurance departments. Additional dozens of companies held high percentages of defaulted real estate, mortgages, and bonds (Townsend 1991).

State Guarantee Funds: Unequal and Unproven

Prior to the savings and loan collapse, most savings and loan deposits were (and continue to be) guaranteed up to $100,000 by the Federal Savings and Loan Insurance Corporation (FSLIC). Depositors throughout the United States were protected by this standing fund and uniform policy backed by the federal government.

When insurance companies fail, however, there is no such federal guarantee for the insured. Protection for policyholders is the responsibility of each state; it is minimally implemented by a state guarantee fund. Generally the guarantee fund is not a standing fund but rather an ad hoc assessment against state licensed insurance companies to help pay claims made on the insolvent insurer. Typically there is a $300,000 cap per claim submitted to the guarantee fund. Claims that are covered by the fund may take years to be paid, and even then the full value of the benefits may never be realized. Ultimately all claims paid out of the state guarantee funds are reflected in higher premiums paid for insurance in the state and often in reduced tax revenues to the state because many states allow fund assessments to be deducted from taxes due. The large burden on the guarantee funds results in part because insurance companies are frequently associated with holding companies that actually control the assets of the insurer. If the insurance company fails, state regulators usually cannot touch assets buried in the holding company. This, of course, is a driving reason behind the existence of holding companies in the insurance industry (U.S. Congress 1989a, 667–668).

Not all state guarantee funds are equal. Some have caps as low as $50,000 on claims submitted to the fund. Five states have no guarantee funds at all for life and health insurance insolvencies (Calif. Establishes Life/Health Guaranty Funds 1991). Twenty states exclude out-of-state policyholders from coverage of a failed insurance company headquartered in the state. Nine states exclude coverage of popular guaranteed investment contracts (GICs), which amount to about $200 billion of life/health insurance industry obligations (Laing 1990). Then there is the problem of state raids on the guarantee funds. During a period of more than a decade, the State of New York transferred $124 million from the property/casualty guarantee fund to the general operating budget. The New York Court of Appeals eventually ruled the transfer unconstitutional, but similar transfers are occurring in other states (N.Y. Court Says State Must Restore Guaranty Fund 1991).

Finally, the whole system of state guarantee funds has never been tested by catastrophic multiple-company, multibillion-dollar failures. It may be tested soon, however. Losses from recent insurer insolvencies are already pushing $20 billion (Welles and Farrell 1989). Many insurers may not have the huge amounts of cash necessary to meet assessments portioned out by state regulators. The resulting fund assessments could push additional companies into insolvency, which would result in a domino effect with unknown consequences for the millions of persons holding health insurance policies with failed life/health companies.

A nonprofit research organization in Durham, North Carolina, recently released the results of a comprehensive study of insurance insolvencies in fifteen southern states and the District of Columbia (Knowles 1990). The Southern Finance Project determined that beginning in 1984 there was a sudden increase in state guarantee fund assessments resulting from insurance insolvencies—a total of fifty-eight insolvencies in the following five years. Currently policyholders and taxpayers in the South are responsible for nearly a billion dollars in losses from these insurance company failures. More astounding, however, is that in a third of these southern states insurers may subtract the total amount assessed by the state guarantee fund from their state taxes. As a result, insolvencies that affected these states during the period 1985–1988 will cost taxpayers more than $220 million. These sums are so enormous that the resulting tax shortfalls are likely to necessitate significant budget cuts or tax increases in several of these states. Currently under consideration are increased sales, property, and use taxes, which will disproportionately affect lower-income households.

State guarantee funds and insurance departments have been so overwhelmed by insolvencies in recent years that a group of receivers and regulators founded the Society of Insurance Receivers (SIRS) in 1991 to coordinate and standardize the way insolvencies are handled nationally. Organization benefits include a regular newsletter and networking opportunities "allowing [members] to swap insurance company insolvency stories." SIRS anticipates a membership of up to 200 by the end of 1992 (Cox 1991).

Perhaps the most appropriate closing statement for this chapter is a quote by Robert McDonald, chief executive officer of LifeUSA, based in Minneapolis. His shockingly candid insider's statement about the life/health insurance industry appeared not too long ago in an issue of *Business Week:* "There are many companies in deep, fundamental trouble. People would be scared if they knew what was happening" (Welles and Farrell 1989, 79).

Summary

Widespread failures in the 1990s among major health insurance carriers will victimize large numbers of people across the nation. The causes for these failures, and the pervasiveness of these causes throughout the industry, reflect a pattern similar in many respects to the savings and loan catastrophe of the 1980s. Vast junk bond holdings, a collapsed real estate market, incompetent or thieving management, lax or corrupt state regulators, and excessive underpricing are some of the main contributing factors to an industrywide pattern of insolvencies. State guarantee funds vary in their ability to protect insurance policyholders from company failures, and the system as a whole may collapse in the face of multiple major insurance company failures.

Every insolvency, however, creates a new constituency of people who better understand the private insurance racket. Many of them will invest time and energy to correct its abuses or eliminate it. Donn Sigerson is a good example. He is a retired California business executive who lost several hundred thousand dollars (which he had intended to use to supplement his retirement income) during the recent multibillion-dollar failure of Executive Life. He started the Executive Life Support Network, which consists of "very angry" people who now hold largely worthless Executive Life policies. Sigerson and his Network members take action by voting and suing (Brostoff 1991b). For obvious reasons, they no longer appreciate the private insurance industry.

chapter eight

The Inefficient Private Sector

> Consider: the Postal Service pays a personal visit, albeit a brief one, to almost every home and office in the country five or six times a week, processes more than 100 *billion* separate pieces of mail each year (no small portion generated by the insurance industry) and, incidentally, runs 30,000 retail "stores" where you can walk in and buy stamps, register letters, apply for passports, send money orders or collect your mail. And it does all that with *one-third* as many people as sell and process the nation's insurance.
>
> —*Andrew Tobias,* The Invisible Bankers

Administrative Costs

In the business of health insurance it is demonstrably untrue that the private sector is more efficient than the public sector. A recent study by Citizen Action, a Washington-based national consumer organization, found that for every dollar paid out in claims by the commercial health insurers, more than $.33 is spent on overhead (Wagner 1990b). This overhead includes bloated administrative salaries, marketing, commissions, and other expenses. In 1985, for example, health insurance overhead cost as much as all expenditures nationwide for health research, new health facility construction, and public health programs combined (Woolhandler and Himmelstein 1989). Contrast this with the government-administered Medicare health insurance program, which has an overhead of 2.3 cents for every dollar paid in claims. Overhead for the federal health insurance program is less than one-fourteenth that of commercial health insurance.

Health care in Canada is provided almost entirely by the private sector, as it is in the United States. And, like physicians in the United States, physicians in Canada practice predominantly on a fee-for-service basis.

The principal difference between the two systems is that commercial health insurers in Canada are not involved with the vast majority of health care provided to the Canadian people because health insurance is a government-administered service. As a result, in Canada for every dollar paid in health insurance claims $.03 is paid for administrative overhead, which is about one-tenth the overhead rate of commercial health insurers in the United States (Wagner 1990b).

A dramatic example of the efficiency of public-sector health insurance is readily apparent in a comparison of private health insurance in Massachusetts with provincial health plans in Canada. Blue Cross/Blue Shield of Massachusetts employs 6,682 workers to administer coverage of 2.7 million insured. All the provincial health plans in Canada combined, covering 25 million insured residents, employ fewer people than the Blues in Massachusetts. In British Columbia, for example, 435 provincial workers administer coverage for more than 3 million residents (Woolhandler and Himmelstein 1991).

A study in the state of Washington by Washington Citizen Action indicated that "it cost commercial insurance companies like Prudential and Aetna $148.9 million more to provide Washington residents with insurance than it would have cost the Canadian system or the Medicare program to provide the same benefits" (Citizen Action Study Exposes 1990, 1). The Washington researchers estimated that 126,000 uninsured Washington residents could be provided health insurance with the money wasted by commercial health insurance overhead in their state.

A recent study by the General Accounting Office evaluated the Canadian health insurance system for "lessons for the United States" on behalf of the Committee on Government Operations, U.S. House of Representatives. The GAO study came to these extraordinary conclusions:

> If the United States were to shift to a system of universal coverage and a single payer, as in Canada, the savings in administrative costs would be more than enough to offset the expense of universal coverage. GAO estimates that, in the short run:
>
> - Savings in insurance overhead would be $34 billion.
> - Savings in hospital and physician administrative costs could be another $33 billion. . . .
> - The cost of serving the newly insured would be about $18 billion.
> - The cost of providing additional services to those currently insured—stemming from elimination of copayments and deductibles—could be about $46 billion.
>
> In the long run, effective limitations on provider payments through global budgeting and negotiated physician fees, as well as controls on expensive technology, could significantly constrain the future growth of U.S. health

spending, leading to substantial further cost savings. (U.S. General Accounting Office 1991a, 6–7)

A study released in summer 1990 by Illinois Public Action (IPAC), a consumer organization, indicated that the commercial health insurance overhead problem is escalating dramatically rather than tapering off. Illinois Public Action found that during the period 1980–1989 insurance company overhead rose at a rate almost twice that of all other medical care costs. Insurers have typically accomplished this by raising their premiums at a faster rate than the actual increasing cost of health care justifies (New Study Blasts Insurance Paperwork 1990).

In large part, as a result of the need to process a deluge of paperwork from hundreds of commercial insurers, administrative expenses for U.S. hospitals in the late 1980s were about 20.2 percent of total expenses. In Canada, however, with the simplified government insurance program, hospital overhead was less than half that—about 9 percent (Woolhandler and Himmelstein 1991). Like hospitals, individual physicians in practice in the United States are also affected by extra expenses related to the dominance of commercial private health insurers. Recently, for example, Victor Fuchs and James Hahn, two well-known medical economists, published an article comparing physician expenditures in the United States with those in Canada (Fuchs and Hahn 1990). They noted that professional overhead for U.S. physicians is 48 percent of all business-related expenditures whereas it is only 34 percent in Canada. Fuchs and Hahn estimated that about 4 percent of the 48 percent ($2.5 billion in 1983) is related to the need to hire personnel to process paperwork related to billing and insurance that Canadian physicians simply do not have to deal with.

There is some evidence that this paperwork itself is a barrier to health care access among those who are insured. A study sponsored by the Southern Legislative Conference and the Southern Governors' Association determined that paperwork associated with some public health insurance programs such as Medicaid confused and discouraged applicants. Hundreds of thousands of deserving applicants for Medicaid and welfare may not have received their benefits because of obstacles involving paperwork. Some of these obstacles included illiteracy, language barriers, and lack of proper documentation (Tolchin 1988). This problem may become more serious as an increasing number of health care providers attempt to cut overhead by requiring the patients themselves (rather than office staff) to fill out insurance forms.

Fuchs and Hahn also found that physicians in the United States spend about twice as much money as their Canadian colleagues for rent, office furnishings, and related office expenses but that only a small part of this difference is attributable to a higher standard of living in the United States: "More important may be the fact that competition for well-insured patients is more intense in the United States, especially among procedure-oriented physicians, many of whom have lower workloads than they desire. Physicians usually do not compete for insured patients by lowering fees, but they can try to attract such patients by offering a higher level of amenities" (Fuchs and Hahn 1990, 889).

Why Insurers Don't Compete by Cutting Costs

A number of years ago, Jon Gabel and Alan Monheit, economists with the National Center for Health Services Research, posed an interesting question (Gabel and Monheit 1983, 623): "Why don't insurers compete more aggressively?" If health insurers were more competitive and more conscious about controlling their costs and the cost of health care for which they paid benefits, then theoretically at least the cost of health insurance would stabilize or decline. Their findings are quite revealing.

According to these researchers, part of the answer to the lack of aggressive competition among commercial health insurers involves "the classic 'free-rider' problem" (Gabel and Monheit 1983, 626). In other words, cost-containment efforts on the part of insurers involve additional expenditures, but other insurers are also likely to benefit with no additional expenditures. In such a case, the passive insurer may emerge in a better competitive position.

For example, some commercial insurers have engaged in utilization review procedures such as requiring a second opinion for surgery, case management, prior authorization, and claims review techniques. All of these utilization review procedures have the ultimate aim of reducing health care expenditures, reducing claims made on the insurer, and ultimately putting the insurer in a more competitive position in the market compared with other insurers who do not engage in such aggressive cost containment. The problem is that planning, instituting, and maintaining these utilization review procedures cost the initiating insurer money but the benefits of such cost-containment efforts tend to spread to all insurers, even those who are free riders, that is, who have not spent money on similar cost-containment programs.

A physician or other health care personnel, for example, may be influenced by an insurer to remind that insurer's clients to get a second opinion for recommended surgery. Health care providers, however, generally are not aware of exactly which insurer is used by each of their patients or what the conditions of that insurance are. For that reason they may simply recommend to all patients under appropriate circumstances to get a second opinion. In this situation the cost-containment efforts of the initial insurer cost a great deal of money but end up benefiting other insurers, many of whom have put few resources into cost containment. Ultimately this sequence of events puts the insurer with the aggressive cost-containment program in a less competitive, rather than a more competitive, situation vis-à-vis other commercial insurers. Consequently, the "most efficient cost containment program for the private insurer, therefore, is not necessarily the same program that is most efficient for society" (Gabel and Monheit 1983, 626).

No Monopsonistic Clout for Commercial Insurers

Gabel and Monheit reviewed the research literature to see how effective commercial insurers have been in negotiating reduced rates with large numbers of physicians and hospitals. They found that Blue Cross/Blue Shield plans had been somewhat effective in negotiating widespread reductions in hospital and physician charges because, unlike regular commercial health insurers, they had regional monopsonies; that is, they were permitted by the states to be the sole purchasers of health care for their customers in specified regions. Generally, however, regular commercial insurers are not successful in negotiating widespread fee reductions with hospitals or physicians because these insurers are not accorded monopsonistic privileges by state regulators. There are dozens, perhaps hundreds, of commercial health insurers operating in a typical state. Because of lack of dominance over the market by any one of these insurers, few if any have the monopsonistic clout of Blue Shield or Blue Cross. As a result, they are not able to effectively implement widespread fee reductions as a significant cost-containment strategy. In any case, it was found that there was little evidence even in the best case that monopsonistic buying power was strong enough to reduce health care costs to all purchasers of health care services in the region.

The buying power of many commercial insurers appears to be sufficient to negotiate reduced fees with a small selection (as opposed to a wide range, as described earlier) of hospitals and physicians as a means of cost containment, and indeed this has been a moderately growing trend in recent years. Here the traditional resistance has focused on the consumer of health insurance. There is a strong desire on the part of the purchasers of health insurance to have the freedom to choose any health care provider and any hospital they prefer for treatment. This consumer preference has delayed but not prevented the massive use of this cost-containment procedure by commercial insurers.

The financial role played by health insurance in the commercial insurance industry is yet another obstacle to aggressive competition among health insurers. For most health insurers, particularly larger multiline health insurers, health insurance is among the least profitable of their various lines of insurance. But it serves as a loss leader: Once insurers sell health insurance policies, it's easier for them to sell other, more profitable, lines of insurance to these same clients.

The principal reason it has traditionally been a low-profit line is that it requires a great deal of liquidity compared with other lines of insurance. Premiums come in on a monthly basis and payments for claims go out on a monthly basis. Compare this with, for instance, life insurance, for which premiums may be paid for decades before there is a claim. Commercial insurers make most of their profits on investment income, and there is more to invest when the benefits are paid out infrequently, like with life insurance, than when benefits are paid out frequently, like with health insurance.

Add to this the fact that a health insurer who wins a new account is likely to have expended resources in order to win that account and having won it will certainly have a number of onetime additional expenses in the first year. Accounts have to be set up, additional administrative expenses and underwriting expenses have to be paid, and so forth.

In summary, in this situation commercial insurers do not want an aggressively competitive market, but rather an "orderly market" for "orderly competition" (Gabel and Monheit 1983, 633). State regulators oblige. Most state insurance regulatory agencies have established a limit to the growth of commercial insurers based on the ratio of new premiums written to the value of total assets. Although the nominal reason for this widespread limit to aggressive growth by commercial insurers is protection against growth-related insolvencies, the practical result in most states is simply orderly competition among commercial health insurers.

Finally, perhaps the most important reason health insurers do not compete aggressively in the marketplace in terms of the cost of premiums is that a large portion of the profits made by the health insurance industry come from investments of premiums. If, as a result of aggressive competition, insurers were forced to compete on the basis of reductions of premiums, the cash coming in for investments would be reduced. This reduction would pose a serious threat to the insurance industry. Their interest lies in an inefficient health care system that results in maximized premiums and cash for investments, not an efficient health care system with reduced premiums and reduced cash for investments.

Summary

The extraordinary wastefulness of the health insurance industry has resulted from special concessions from government, a cartel-like organization, extremely high administrative costs, and decades of expanding business. The distribution and administration of comparable forms of health insurance in the public sector cost a small fraction of what they do in the private sector. There is little incentive in the commercial health insurance industry to become more efficient because it frequently makes no sense from a corporate cost-benefit point of view. In addition, crucial investment income is dependent on high levels of cash flow from premiums. Any efficiencies that might result in declining premium income would also result in declining cash for investments and hence declining investment income. This outcome is patently against the interests of health insurers.

chapter nine

A Political Question: Accommodation, Compromise, or Struggle?

Theodore Roosevelt talked about it in 1912 when he ran for president under the Bull Moose Party. Harry Truman called for it in a speech to Congress in 1945. And Sen. Edward Kennedy (D-Mass.) proposed it in a bill in 1969 and has done so every year since.

None of their proposals for national health insurance were ever adopted—or even got as far as a floor vote in Congress.

—David Zinman

Proposed National Health Legislation and the Role of Private Health Insurance

As of early 1991 President George Bush and his administration had been riding high on the multibillion-dollar "victory" in Iraq and had not yet felt the full political brunt of tens of millions of American people without access to rudimentary health care. Health and Human Services secretary Louis W. Sullivan had firmly committed the Bush administration to no national health insurance program and, indeed, no structural changes in the health care system whatsoever (Pullen 1991b). Near the end of 1991, however, Secretary Sullivan did concede to a secretive meeting with leaders of the health insurance industry. They discussed how the industry might reduce a few billion dollars of administrative costs by "innovative" approaches such as increasing the use of computers in billing and record keeping (Mesche 1991).

Additional hints about the administration's views on the ongoing crisis in health care emerged in the budget reconciliation proposals. Bush would reduce Medicare funding by $23 billion over five years and begin the process to introduce means testing for Medicare, that is, qualifying for it on the basis of income and assets. He would take funds from community health centers and maternal and child health programs and shift them to services for pregnant women. He would take money from school lunch programs and shift it to women, infant, and children (WIC) supplemental food programs. Finally, he would make cuts in existing programs for the needy that provide respiratory and physical therapy and durable medical equipment. The accompanying recommendation is that these needs be met by private insurance (Health Care as a Basic Right 1991). Clearly, then, there is no sensible administration plan to deal with growing obstacles to health care in the United States. Congress occasionally does better.

In summer 1991 Senate Democratic leaders introduced the national health insurance plan favored by the Democrats. It has no surprises and accommodates the needs of the health insurance industry and other profitable interests. It appears to be incapable of containing cost or assuring quality. Employers would have to provide employees a minimum health insurance package. If they failed to do so, they would pay additional payroll tax into a public system that would insure employees. State-mandated benefits would be eliminated, much to the joy of commercial insurers. Small businesses would get certain tax breaks, and insurers would be required to minimize medical underwriting and to provide community-based rating (i.e., the same insurance rate for everyone). A broader health insurance plan would replace Medicaid. A new federal agency would conduct medical outcome research and develop guidelines for physicians and other health care providers (Brostoff 1991a). A few other proposals that have had some popularity from different constituents follow.

The Basic Health Benefits for All Americans Act

This proposal offers more of the same with a little tinkering in some areas. Under this act, more Americans would be covered by health insurance but the structure of health care services and financing that caused the problems in the first place would be retained. The role of private insurers would be expanded. This act is sponsored by Senator Edward Kennedy as S. 768 and by Congressman Henry Waxman as H.R. 1845. It would expand Medicaid to cover the poor and near-poor and leave Medicare in place to cover the elderly. Employers would be required to use private health insurance to cover employees. Others not covered by these mechanisms would be eligible for federal- or state-subsidized insurance coverage. The health care delivery system would remain unchanged. The minimum health benefits package would be rudimentary, allowing up to $3,000 per family for out-of-pocket expenses as copayments, premiums, and deductibles. Financing of this proposal would build on current financing strategies. Employers would pay most of the health insurance costs for employees. Small employers might qualify for subsidies and could join private pools operated by the private insurance sector. Under this act, private health insurance would be heavily relied upon; however, exclusions from coverage because of health status or preexisting conditions would not be allowed (U.S. Congress 1990c).

The USHealth Act

This act would bring health insurance to more Americans but would leave the faulty health care delivery system intact. Existing federal health insurance programs would be enlarged to serve the entire population, but the insurance industry would be given a broad parasitic role to play. Rep. Edward Roybal from California is the sponsor of the USHealth Act, H.R. 2980. The act would greatly expand Medicare and would be administered by an enlarged and renamed Health Care Financing Administration. The resulting program would replace Medicare, Medicaid, and private health insurance plans. However, a key role would be reserved for private health insurers as contractors with the government to review and process billing. This is similar to the fraud-plagued role now occupied by insurers on contract with the government to administer Medicare and Medicaid. Allowable benefits are more comprehensive than, for example, under the Basic Health Benefits for All Americans Act, but these benefits could be severely curtailed under cost-cutting procedures outlined in the act. For families above federal poverty level, cost sharing of 20 to 25 percent is a centerpiece of the cost-containment effort. In addition, there is a prospective payment plan to be negotiated with some providers, and a cap on the costs of the entire program at 12 percent of the GNP. The system would be financed primarily by payroll taxes, premiums, employer taxes, and income taxes (U.S. Congress 1990c).

The Pepper Commission

The U.S. Bipartisan Commission on Comprehensive Health Care, commonly called the Pepper Commission, was established toward the end of 1989 to develop a strategy to deal with the health care crisis. The commission, composed of members of Congress and presidential appointees, released its report the following year. Commission recommendations were not particularly innovative; they reflected a number of concepts that had already received wide exposure. These included some cost-containment efforts, publicly funded long-term care benefits, mandatory health insurance at the place of employment, public funding for health insurance for the poor and unemployed, and tinkering with the market to make health insurance more affordable to small businesses (Support for National Health Care 1989; Wagner 1990a). These recommendations were introduced as the Pepper Health Care Bill mid-1991 by Sen. John Rockefeller (D-W. Va.) and Rep. Henry Waxman (D-Calif.) (Universal Health Care Bill Introduced 1991). As an analyst in one of the major insurance industry newsletters observed, "The Pepper Commission's recommendations open new and expanded markets for private insurers" (Kluepfel 1990).

The Universal Health Care Act

This proposal for a single-payer, universal-access health insurance system was introduced by Rep. Marty Russo (D-Ill.), vice-chair of the Subcommittee on Health of the House Ways and Means Committee. It is self-consciously modeled on the Canadian system and is widely supported in Congress and by labor as well as other organizations. It covers physician and hospital care, long-term care, mental health, prescription drugs, dental services, and preventive services. There are no copayments or deductibles. The plan would be financed through state and federal contributions, payroll taxes, and personal and corporate income taxes. Administrative wastes would be cut throughout the system as a result of the use of the single-payer plan; however, private insurers might be used to process claims. National and state budgets would control costs. Practice guidelines would attempt to curtail the delivery of excessive medical services (Russo 1991).

The U.S. Health Service Act

Rep. Ron Dellums of California has repeatedly introduced this bill (currently H.R. 3229) into Congress since the mid-1970s. This act would establish a national health service that would replace all current federal health insurance and health care programs and nearly all private health insurance, private health care providers, and private health care facilities with a community-controlled, federally financed system. All health services would be available to all residents free of charge. Nearly all providers would be civil servants, providing care as a service rather than as a way of generating wealth. The private health insurance industry would have no significant role whatsoever. The national health service would be financed by funds currently paid into federal health programs and by shifting current employer payments for private health insurance to payments for the national health service. Additional sources of income such as corporate and individual income taxes would be implemented. Cost containment would be effectively achieved by permanently eliminating hundreds of billions of dollars of medically unnecessary costs in the insurance and medical industries such as profit, commissions, excessive administrative salaries and perks, overutilization of expensive high-tech medical equipment, and fee-for-service practice leading to excessive medical procedures (U.S. Congress 1989d).

State Health Legislation and the Role of Private Health Insurance

Despite, or perhaps because of, inaction at the federal level, there has been significant activity among the states in attempting to control health care costs and improve accessibility. Hawaii leaped ahead of all the others in 1974 when it established a law requiring that employers provide minimum health insurance benefits to full-time employees (Zinman 1990). This plan makes extensive use of private health insurers and was the model used for the proposed national Basic Health Benefits for All Americans Act (Kluepfel 1990). After a lengthy period of relative quiescence among the states, the mid-1980s witnessed a burst of state initiatives. In 1987 *Health Care News,* for example, published by the activist group National Health Care Campaign, reported on pertinent developments in "27 state campaigns." Some of the modest victories scattered across the nation were gains such as expansion of Medicaid, enactment of antidumping regulations, establishment of programs to cover some of the uninsured, and improvement of the quality of nursing home care (National Health Care Campaign 1987). Modest gains in the future, however, may be giving way to substantial structural reform at the state level. In 1990 only two state legislatures considered a single-payer, universal-access health insurance system modeled on that of Canada. The following year, at least thirteen additional state legislatures gave a Canadian-type universal health insurance system serious consideration. All these proposals involve publicly funded plans that prohibit significant involvement of private health insurers (Insurance Canadian-Style 1991).

In spring 1990 the New York State Health Department in conjunction with the School of Public Health at the State University of New York at Albany sponsored the first conference for states that focused on the issue of universal health care. The two-day affair was attended by representatives from twenty-seven states. Featured events included speakers from the states of Hawaii, Massachusetts, and Washington who described programs controlling health care costs and broadening accessibility in their respective states (Zinman 1990). A couple of months after the conference the new chair of the National Governors' Association, Washington governor Booth Gardner, gave the first speech in his new capacity. He announced that he had selected health care as the primary focus of his tenure as chair of the association and reportedly called the issue "'a national scandal,' . . . a complex form of anarchy that is 'rapidly degenerating into just plain chaos'" (New Head of National Governors' Assn.

Advocates 1990, 4). At about the same time, Republican and Democratic governors were giving testimony before the Senate Finance Panel's subcommittee on the uninsured. There was fairly unanimous agreement that the feds have to take the lead role. Governor Michael Dukakis (D-Mass.) observed that " 'fifty health experiments won't give us the kind of national guarantees that our citizens deserve' " (Governors Ask for Federal Action 1990).

> The insurance industry is vitally interested in the details of state initiatives to broaden access to health care services and to contain costs. In Connecticut, for example, the Special Health Care Plan was implemented in spring 1990. This law created a new reinsurance process so that extra costs to insure higher-risk workers would be distributed among all insurers in the state. Insurers who cover small groups have to contribute to the state high-risk reinsurance pool an amount equal to at least 5 percent of the premiums collected in order to keep the pool solvent. The state's Blue Cross/Blue Shield insurer, carrying a disproportionate amount of small-business health insurance, may be liable for 50 percent of all losses exceeding the amount in the state high-risk reinsurance pool. As a result, the Blues are contemplating a strategy to insure fewer small businesses and shift more of them to the state high-risk pool (Kenkel 1990a).

In Oklahoma more than one out of every five residents are uninsured. Legislation enacted in 1990 established the Oklahoma Basic Health Benefits Board to subsidize small employers and their employees interested in purchasing health insurance. The original bill sought to establish a plan financed and operated directly by the state to contract with health care service providers. The efficiency of this arrangement cut into the profits of private health insurers. The industry successfully lobbied to create a new level of expensive, unnecessary bureaucracy. The legislation now calls for "private firms" to finance and deliver the new state services (Kenkel 1990a).

The optimistically named Illinois Comprehensive Health Insurance Plan began functioning mid-1989. It actually insures only a few percent of the state's uninsured via a tightly capped state high-risk health insurance pool. Most of the nineteen other states with such high-risk pools assess private insurers to keep the pool solvent. In Illinois the residents rather than the insurance industry directly bear this burden. All the pool's subsidies come directly from the Illinois General Revenue Fund. Adding insult to injury, Mutual of Omaha Insurance Company is contracted to administer the plan (Kluepfel 1990).

The Health Care Security Act of the State of Massachusetts was originally passed in 1988 but has been delayed and amended several times since then because of lobbying by the business sector. The plan would subsidize the cost of health insurance paid by employers while relying heavily on the existing system of private insurers. Recent changes in the law do not require businesses to comply with its major provisions until 1993. Currently, however, the state Department of Medical Security has developed a special working relationship with John Hancock Insurance Company to collect small amounts of money from employers to subsidize an insurance pool for the uninsured (Kluepfel 1990).

The State of New York has been working for several years on Universal New York Health Care, popularly called UNYCare. The plan would derive its principal funding from general revenues, initially from existing state bad debt and charity health insurance pools. As it expanded it would pick up additional funds from employer and employee contributions and subsidize small businesses that provided health insurance to employees. Despite superficial similarities to this point with some other state plans, UNYCare has a few features that make it quite distinct. In order to save administrative and medical services costs, this plan would establish a single-payer system (i.e., a single payer for health care services) operated by the state or a contractor. The single-payer authority would negotiate with providers to establish fixed rates and with insurers to provide standardized minimum benefits to encourage them to compete on the basis of price. In an apparent accommodation with the commercial insurance industry's political clout, UNYCare would contract with private insurers to sell state-approved policies. Clearly this accommodation injects a completely unnecessary layer of bureaucracy into the plan with the result that critical funds would be siphoned away from the provision of health care services (Kluepfel 1990; New York Department of Health 1990).

The American Public Health Association

The American Public Health Association (APHA) is the largest professional public health association in the United States, with about 50,000 members in affiliates nationwide. In 1976 the president of APHA somberly announced in his regular column in the association's monthly newspaper that "as a result of a resolution passed by the Governing Council, APHA is now on record as endorsing a National Health Service (NHS) rather than National Health Insurance (NHI)" (Pickett 1976, 2). A national health service has neither public nor private health insurance but provides health care directly through publicly salaried providers in public facilities. Rep. Ron Dellums's U.S. Health Service Act described earlier is such a plan.

In response to a reawakened national interest in the issue, the APHA executive committee developed and agreed upon the "Sense of the

Congress Resolution" early in 1989, around which they intended to attract significant congressional support. The resolution listed thirteen points summarizing the history of APHA's principles for a national health program. A few months later the executive committee released a pamphlet listing twelve of the thirteen principles. "Affirmative action in the training, employment and promotion of Health Workers" had been dropped (American Public Health Association 1989c). The process of political dilution had begun. The remaining twelve principles for a national health program appeared on the pamphlet as follows:

- Coverage for everyone in the U.S.
- Comprehensive benefits
- Elimination of financial barriers to care
- Financing based on ability to pay
- Publicly accountable administration with a major role for governmental health agencies
- Quality and efficiency assurances
- Fair payment to providers which encourages appropriate treatment by providers and appropriate utilization by consumers
- Ongoing evaluation and planning with consumer and provider participation
- Disease prevention and health promotion programs
- Education, training, and affirmative action for health workers
- Non-discrimination in the delivery of health services
- Education of consumers about their health rights and responsibilities (American Public Health Association 1989b)

The question of private health insurance was not directly addressed in the brochure. However, in the earlier "Sense of the Congress Resolution," a statement denigrating "profit making" in health care combined with the explicitly preferred "major role" of the public sector implied that there would be little or no role for commercial health insurance in a reform package consistent with the APHA resolution.

In fall 1989, at the APHA annual conference, a petition supporting APHA's "Sense of the Congress Resolution" was widely distributed and endorsed by the membership. The petition was initiated by nine past presidents of the organization. It urged the governing council and executive board to develop and advocate its own legislation based on the thirteen principles. APHA leadership negotiated with AFL/CIO to develop a unified position for introduction by Representative Waxman (D-Calif.) but in the process watered down or deleted several of the original thirteen principles. The resulting resolution was considerably less clear about the possible role of private health insurance in a national health program. By August 1990 the revised Sense of the Congress had found a sponsor in Representative Waxman and dozens of cosponsors among Democratic representatives (National Health Resolution Gaining 1990).

In a joint APHA executive board and staff effort earlier in 1989, the original thirteen criteria were systematically applied to a selection of proposed national health programs including

1. Physicians for a National Health Program
2. A Consumer-Choice Health Plan for the 1990s (Enthoven and Kronick)
3. A Progressive Proposal for a National Medical Care System (Milton Terris et. al.)
4. Massachusetts Health Security Program
5. U.S. Health Service Act
6. Basic Health Benefits for All Americans Act
7. Health Security Partnership (Committee for National Health Insurance)
8. For the Health of a Nation (National Leadership Commission on Health Care)

The somewhat controversial draft document scored Rep. Ron Dellums's (D-Calif.) U.S. Health Service Act and Dr. Milton Terris's A Progressive Proposal for a National Medical Care System far ahead of the other contending proposals in terms of how closely they conformed with APHA's thirteen principles (American Public Health Association 1989a). Dellums's U.S. Health Service Act is described earlier in this chapter. Terris's Progressive Proposal includes many of the public national health insurance elements of a Canadian system combined with payments only to provider organizations rather than individual practitioners. Provider organizations would have the status of public utilities and would therefore be under significant public scrutiny and quality control. The system would be mainly federally funded through progressive income taxes. The entire population would be covered with no charge to users for service (Council on Medical Care 1989).

Physicians and Nurses

The American Medical Association (AMA), with over 270,000 members, is the largest and historically most powerful professional organization for U.S. physicians. In summer 1989 the 433 members of the AMA House of Delegates endorsed a tepid proposal advocating that the federal government expand Medicaid and require employers to provide private health insurance to employees. The proposal referred only to full-time employees of large firms and additionally specified that tax credits should ease the burden of additional expenses for business. In the words of a *New York Times* reporter, "The association's action is part of its effort to combat moves to nationalize the health care system in the United States" (Mandatory Insurance Is Backed 1989, A17[L]). The AMA in recent years has pulled out all stops to defeat national health insurance, which the association commonly refers to as "socialized medicine."

> During a 15-month period ending in March 1990, the AMA ranked second on the election commission's list of the top 50 PACs in amount of receipts, [and] second in total spending. . . .
>
> In the 1988 Congressional elections, the AMA spent $5.3-million, including $2.3-million in direct contributions to House and Senate candidates. From January 1989 through March of [1990] it has given money to 348 members of Congress, including eight of the 12 Congressional members of the Pepper Commission. . . .
>
> To replenish its coffers, the AMA embarked on a special effort last year to discredit the Canadian health-care system. . . . [T]he AMA wrote to member physicians. . . . Enough doctors sent checks that the AMA was able to buy ads disparaging the Canadian system in major magazines. (The Crisis in Health Insurance 1990, 609)

State medical associations materially and ideologically extend the political influence of the AMA considerably. For example, during a period of approximately one year ending in March 1990 medical associations in just ten states spent over $4 million supporting their favorite candidates (The Crisis in Health Insurance 1990).

American College of Physicians

The 68,000-member American College of Physicians (ACP) is the largest medical specialty organization in the United States. During their 1990 annual meeting in Chicago, the ACP, much to the chagrin of the AMA, called for a "universal access to health insurance program" that would radically restructure health care in the United States. ACP leaders have criticized the AMA proposal as "'tinkering' and 'patchwork measures' that may be useful short-term strategies for expanding access but will not eliminate serious flaws in the health care system" (Phillips 1990, 14).

The ACP position paper was developed by subcommittees of the ACP Health and Public Policy Committee and was approved by the board of regents in early 1990. The document harshly assails excessive administrative costs and paperwork associated with current reliance on private health insurers:

> A universal access plan could achieve substantial savings by reducing the amount of administrative expenses currently borne by physicians, hospitals, nursing homes, and others providing and paying for health care services.

> Aggregate savings could be achieved by reducing the paperwork and expenses involved in coding for services, billing and collecting payments from patients, and submitting and documenting claims to multiple insurance carriers—each with its own forms, coverage provisions, copayments and deductibles, and review and compliance requirements. Further savings could be achieved by eliminating much of the administrative overhead that health insurance carriers incur for administration, marketing, reserves, and profits. (Ginsburg and Prout 1990, 657)

The ACP position paper does not specify exactly which type of universal access to health insurance program is advocated; however, the position paper refers favorably to several existing systems such as those in Canada, Sweden, Switzerland, and France. The authors of the position paper noted that "national health insurance programs can be operated solely by the government or can be structured to incorporate private health insurance."

Physicians for a National Health Program

Physicians for a National Health Program (PNHP) currently has well over 3,000 physician members. This organization advocates a system for the United States very much like the Canadian system, complete with the abolishment of private health insurance, the establishment of a single-government purchaser of health care, and the retention of private health care providers and facilities. The appearance of the PNHP proposal in the *New England Journal of Medicine* in early 1989 gave the organization considerable initial visibility and legitimacy, which have been maintained since then. Some of the major features of the proposed national health program will

> (1) fully cover everyone under a single, comprehensive public insurance program; (2) pay hospitals and nursing homes a total (global) annual amount to cover all operating expenses; (3) fund capital costs through separate appropriations; (4) pay for physicians' services and ambulatory services in any of three ways: through fee-for-service payments with a simplified fee schedule and mandatory acceptance of the national health program payment as the total payment for a service or procedure (assignment), through global budgets for hospitals and clinics employing salaried physicians, or on a per capita basis (capitation); (5) be funded, at least initially, from the same sources as at present, but with all payments disbursed from a single pool; and (6) contain costs through savings on billing and bureaucracy, improved health planning, and the ability of the national health program, as the single payer for services, to establish overall spending limits. (Himmelstein et al. 1989, 102)

The American Medical Association and the private insurance industry do not support the PNHP proposal. Nevertheless, proposals for plans with concepts similar to the PNHP proposal have been introduced in about half a dozen states. Furthermore, PNHP has been working directly with labor unions such as the Oil, Chemical, and Atomic Workers (OCAW) and has influenced others (Colatosti 1990).

Physicians Forum

Finally, the Physicians Forum is a compact but persistent organization of politically progressive physicians. In existence since the early 1940s, it was first a defender of the principles of national health insurance and in later years of a national health service. "To reverse the trend toward a health care system controlled by profit-driven corporate providers," the forum advocates a national health service along the lines of Dellums's U.S. Health Service Act (Lear 1989; The Health Care Crisis 1985).

Nursing's National Health Proposal

In early 1991 a coalition of eighteen major nursing organizations publicly released Nursing's National Health Proposal. The coalition includes the National League for Nursing, American Nurses Association, American Association of Colleges of Nursing, Oncology Nursing Society, National Association of School Nurses, Inc., American Association of Critical Care Nurses, and Association of Community Health Nursing Educators.

According to an early release of their proposal:

> The Nurses' approach builds on the existing system. We have opted to rearrange existing players, include new incentives to contain costs, and decrease the emphasis on in-patient acute care; placing a new emphasis on prevention, primary care and long-term care services. In the Plan, nurses are positioned as primary caregivers (along with physicians) providing basic health services in all settings. . . .
>
> This proposal supports a private sector approach to continuous quality improvement that is consumer-oriented, closely coordinated with a Federal system that assures minimum standards and a system of enforcement. (Nursing Introduces Its National Health Strategy 1991)

The proposal includes a federally defined minimum health care package financed and delivered through public and private sectors, a much larger role for nurses as providers, and additional resources focused on pregnant women, infants, and children. No specific mention is made of the private health insurance industry, but it appears as though it would flourish under this plan.

Organized Labor, Health Care Reform, and the Role of Private Health Insurance

In fall 1990 the nation's largest umbrella group for organized labor, the AFL-CIO, launched a $4 million media campaign to promote a list of general principles for national health care reform but endorsed no particular program or piece of legislation (Unions Yes 1990). This campaign was closely followed by the October 3 Health Care Action Day; on this day union members nationwide joined in lunchtime demonstrations and picketed nonunion firms not offering health benefits. In addition, a series of nationwide AFL-CIO hearings followed to highlight the national plight of workers with no or inadequate health insurance (Health Care "Action Day" 1990).

An editorial in the progressive publication *The Nation* bemoans the indecisive approach to health care reform legislation by AFL-CIO leadership. The editorial asserts that "Kirkland does not want to commit to any specific plan or piece of legislation until he knows that it has sufficient backing from business and other groups to pass" (Unions Yes 1990, 260).

An article originally published in *Labor Notes,* "a union policy journal," and reprinted in *Allegro,* the Local 802 newsletter out of New York, appears to agree with *The Nation*'s editorial: "Don't look to the AFL-CIO for help. They're playing their usual game of conciliation, backing off any push for wholesale reform before the real bargaining has ever begun" (McClure 1990, 11).

The author of the *Labor Notes* article, Laura McClure, pointed out that Service Employees International union president John Sweeney is head of the AFL-CIO Health-Care Committee and has been a member of the National Leadership Commission on Health Care. The commission was funded by support from corporate manufacturing and insurance interests and included among its members influential individuals associated with manufacturing and insurance corporations, the American Medical Association, organized labor, and other sectors of American political economy. A major report issued by the commission in 1989 included mild recommendations for tort reform, financial incentives for employers to provide health insurance to employees, and fees to be charged most workers and employers to pay for health insurance for the unemployed (Brostoff 1990b). McClure is concerned that corporate interests in health care reform are opposed to labor interests and that AFL-CIO leadership is being unduly influenced by the corporations. Corporate interests involve shifting costs to workers via a "taxpayer bailout of our current health-care system," which she correctly described as "one of the world's most costly and inefficient." She continues by asking: "Why is our health-care system so expensive? Because we have two gigantic, parasitic industries to pay for: the private health-insurance business and the private health care delivery system. And corporations are strongly opposed to any plan that would kill these industries" (McClure 1990).

The National Leadership Commission on Health Care has reportedly been reorganized as the National Leadership Coalition on Health Care Reform, a membership organization rather than an organization of individuals, as it was previously. The coalition claims to have no insurance industry representation but retains most of the principles formerly involved. The coalition's executive director has noted that the coalition is not committed to national health insurance but is open to a variety of options (Brostoff 1990b).

Some Unions Take the Lead

Despite McClure's criticisms of AFL-CIO leadership on the issue of health reform, an important segment of that leadership clearly understands the role of the commercial insurance industry. Edward Cleary, president of the New York State AFL-CIO, gave the keynote speech at the New York State AFL-CIO biennial convention. He explained in unambiguous terms the destructive social impact of the insurance industry as a whole:

> In New York State it is the insurance industry that is the greatest obstacle to progressive new laws. Whether in blocking a Workers' Compensation bill or trying to derail progress toward universal health care, the private insurance carriers are the never-failing source of most of our woes. These parasitic, selfish interests not only care nothing about the hundreds of thousands of workers mangled in industrial accidents, they bilk thousands of the state's employers with exorbitant premiums. They are a cartel. The OPEC oil cartel and the Medellin drug cartel could learn a few monopolistic tricks from the New York insurance cartel. They zealously cherish their privileged positions, secured by the corruptions of the political system. (Cleary Calls for Economic Reform 1990, 6)

Some unions have taken a strong stance somewhat independently of AFL-CIO leadership on the issue of health care reform. The United Auto Workers union, for example, has supported the AFL-CIO's nationwide lobbying efforts and demonstrations but has gone further to publicly endorse a "national health program similar to Canada's system" (High Insurance Costs 1990). The Canadian system involves a publicly funded health insurance system operated on the basis of a federal/provincial partnership. However, most medical services remain in the private sector. All health care is available at little or no cost to Canadian residents. Funding is derived mainly through various taxes, and private health insurers are prohibited from selling insurance for services already provided by the government. It is not surprising that the Canadian system operates with a fraction of the administrative overhead plaguing the American system. Cost containment enforced by the federal and provincial buyers of health care services has been far more effective than in the United States. Finally, opinion polls indicate that Canadians like their health care system much better than Americans like theirs (Canadians Like Their System 1990).

Gerald McEntee, head of the American Federation of State, County, and Municipal Employees (AFSCME), was one of the leaders of organized labor who announced the AFL-CIO's nationwide rallies for health care reform at the kickoff press conference. Despite McEntee's association with AFL-CIO's less specific policy statement, AFSCME District Council 37 has formulated a detailed health care reform strategy based on the Canadian model. According to an article written in District Council 37's newsletter by Glenna Michaels, a health policy consultant for the District Council:

> The union's plan is a single, unified national program for everyone.
>
> Every person would be guaranteed access to medical care services by a single insurance plan administered by a single public agency with opportunity for participation by labor and consumers.
>
> A comprehensive set of health care benefits would be available to everyone in the U.S. regardless of where they live. Patients would be entitled to care at hospitals, doctor's offices or clinics of their choice.
>
> Patients would not be billed for care but would pay once through a tax or premium contribution. All employers would be required to contribute to the cost of health benefits. Unions would bargain for full employer payment of the benefit package and for additional benefits.
>
> Hospitals would receive a global annual budget for all operating costs; capital funds for equipment, expansion and renovation would be separate.
>
> Physicians would be paid on a fee-for-service, per patient or salaried basis. (Michaels 1990, 8)

A number of union officers and AFL-CIO officials hold positions in the Committee for National Health Insurance (CNHI) and the Health Security Action Council (HSAC). The committee was founded in 1968 to reform the organization and financing of health care in the United States. CNHI's leadership and members "comprise a cross-section of America, representing labor, business, women, youth, senior citizens, education, religious and farm organizations" (Health Security Action Council 1988). The council is a network of organizations with a consitutency reflecting the individual membership of the committee. These two organizations advocate a plan called the Health Security Partnership. Under this plan, basic benefits are established by the federal government, but organization, administration, and financing would be undertaken primarily at the state or territorial level. A proliferation of state-qualified and approved private health insurance plans is envisioned. The plan "encourages private insurers and providers to be part of the administration of the program" (The Health Security Partnership, n.d., 5).

AFL-CIO Health Care Committee Deadlock

The emerging split among major labor unions regarding the national health care question revealed itself during an important January 31, 1991, meeting of the AFL-CIO Health Care Committee:

> Committee Chair John Sweeney of the SEIU [Service Employees International Union], moving his own motion for the AFL-CIO to adopt an employer-based, "limited-payer" regulatory reform, was supported by Lane Kirkland's top legislative and policy aides, and gained the votes of Robert Georgine (Building and Construction Trades), Jack Joyce (Bricklayers), Al Shanker (AFT), Lynn Williams (USWA), Lenore Miller (RWDSU), and Richard Kilroy (TCU). Sweeny voted a proxy for William Wynn (UFCW), which had been obtained only to support a "consensus" position, according to Jay Foreman, executive vice-president of the UFCW.
>
> Opposing Sweeney, and supporting a "single-payer" social insurance health system as the AFL-CIO's position in the national health care debate, were Gerald McEntee (AFSCME), Richard Trumka (UMWA), Owen Beiber (UAW), Morton Bahr (CWA), Jack Sheinkman (ACTWU), George Kourpias (IAM), Moe Biller (APWU), and Jay Mazur (ILGWU). (Labor Research Association 1991)

The motion was lost as a result of an 8–8 tie. Next, Richard Trumka of the United Mine Workers proposed that the AFL-CIO adopt a position supporting a single-payer health insurance system. It also was defeated on the basis on an 8–8 tie vote.

Kirkland Addresses the AMA

There was no hint of the fundamental rift in the Health Care Committee three and one-half weeks later on February 17, when AFL-CIO president Lane Kirkland addressed the American Medical Association National Leadership Conference. This address took place only a couple of days before the final draft emerged of the AFL-CIO executive council's position paper, "National Health Care Reform." Key points in the address gave a clear picture of what was to emerge from the AFL-CIO executive council a few dozen hours later:

> For the first time in history, organized labor and organized medicine are headed in the same direction on the issue of national health care reform.
>
> As Dr. Tupper emphasized in his testimony before an AFL-CIO regional hearing last fall in San Francisco, there are striking similarities between the AMA's "Health Access America" proposal and the elements of our grassroots campaign for national health care reform. . . .
>
> We in labor now find ourselves in common cause not only with the AMA, but with many of our traditional adversaries in the business community—including the National Association of Manufacturers and some of the nation's biggest corporations.
>
> For our part, a new sense of pragmatism seems to be taking hold. For example, a few years ago, who among you could have imagined a difference of opinion within the AFL-CIO's own Health Care Committee on whether or not to pursue a Canadian-style single-payor program?
>
> But that is indeed what has happened in our deliberative process. And it's only one measure of our determination to be realistic in the debate over national health care reform. This time, we intend to see real health care reform enacted into law. (Kirkland 1991, 1–2)

Kirkland found common ground with the AMA, the National Association of Manufacturers, and major corporations because he borrowed his ideas about health care reform from the corporate-dominated National Leadership Coalition for Health Care Reform. These ideas are more clearly reflected in the AFL-CIO executive council's "National Health Care Reform" (National Health Care Reform 1991). Some of the major health care reforms called for in this document include

- a federal authority to negotiate uniform reimbursement rates with hospitals and providers
- a core package of benefits
- "administrative intermediaries" (private insurance companies) to standardize claims forms
- dropping Medicare eligibility to age sixty
- informing physicians about practice guidelines
- encouraging physicians to avoid unnecessary tests and medical procedures
- devising a strategy to provide long-term care (National Health Care Reform 1991)

The working people of America lost a great deal in this historical capitulation to corporate and provider interests. Yet the real battle had not even begun.

Business, Health Care Reform, and Private Health Insurance

Business leaders are not warming executive rockers waiting for health care reform to happen. In the past few years they have taken an active stance through both existing and new trade organizations representing their interests. In general they want to reduce the escalating costs they pay for employee health care benefits; however, business interests are not necessarily unified in terms of what this means or how to get there:

> Big companies that provide health insurance desperately want to shuffle the costs of employment-based benefits to workers (through employee contributions or concessions); to consumers (through higher prices); to other industries and firms and direct competitors (through federally mandated insurance); or to all of the above (through tax-financed national health insurance). For employers, "national health care" is a catch phrase for any political means of escaping health care liabilities and the high costs of private insurance. (Gordon 1991, 376)

Earlier in this chapter there was a discussion of the industry-initiated National Leadership Commission on Health Care, reconstituted as the National Leadership Coalition on Health Care Reform. Another industry organization, the Washington Business Group on Health, has approximately 200 corporate members. They, and the 13,500 corporate members of the long-standing National Association of Manufacturers (NAM), appear to be slowly moving in the direction of accepting more government control of the U.S. health care system. An interesting observation by Willis Goldbeck, past president of the Washington Business Group, was that an important common denominator among comparatively less expensive European health care systems is that they are not based on private health insurance (Intelligent Investing in Health Care 1991; Freudenheim 1989a). It is not clear, however, to what extent this thinking pervades the remaining membership of NAM or the Washington Business Group. This question is particularly important in light of the fact that insurance companies hold huge amounts of stocks and bonds for major corporations. The top fifty insurance companies in 1988 held $58 billion worth. It seems reasonable to assume that corporate chiefs will be less than enthusiastic to call for the elimination of part of an industry that provides them with vast sums of capital (Labor Research Association 1989).

A representative for the National Federation of Independent Business, a trade group of small businesses, made it clear that although health care concerns are top priority, approaches relying on mandated benefits are taboo. However, this does not necessarily mean that more government involvement is taboo. A nationwide survey of 565 presidents of small companies indicated that 38 percent were in favor of national health insurance, 39 percent against, and the rest undecided. At the Business Roundtable, an organization composed of corporate chief executives, the chair of the task force on health issues is the president of the Metropolitan Life Insurance Company. It should come as no surprise that this group supports tax incentives to help individuals and businesses purchase private health insurance (Freudenheim 1989a).

Some industry leaders have been striking out on their own, testing waters outside the confines of trade organization health policy compromises. Lee Iacocca has discussed in a very positive light "a national health insurance program for the U.S." Other business leaders such as Art Puccini, a vice-president at General Electric, and Robert Mercer, former Goodyear board member, have expressed similar sentiments. Walter B. Maher, director of employee benefits at Chrysler, has waxed eloquent about the Canadian health care system in particular—a national health care system in which the private health insurance industry plays no significant role (Freudenheim 1989b; Gordon 1991). Bethlehem Steel Corporation and the United Steelworkers signed a contract in mid-1989 in which they agreed to "'develop and support an appropriate national health policy, which will assure essential care to all citizens, control health care costs and equitably distribute those costs' across the economy" (Freudenheim 1989a, D11).

A note of caution. Industry's enthusiasm for a stronger federal role in the health care system may hide more than the obvious self-serving agenda. In an interview with a *New York Times* business reporter, Ralph Pollack, chief operating officer of a multicompany employee health care plan, candidly admitted that companies are looking for a scapegoat on which to blame health care rationing decisions. In the words of the *Times* reporter, "If a heart patient were to die and the family were to attribute the death to the failure to authorize a bypass operation, then the blame would fall not on the patient's employer, but on the mandatory government standards" (Uchitelle 1990, D2).

The Insurance Industry and Health Care Reform

Health insurers are acutely aware that major changes are occurring in their industry and that additional massive change is imminent. Sometimes their public response to this seems pathetically chaotic and hopelessly ineffective in terms of protecting their own interests, not to mention the health care of the American public. However, behind the public facade the industry has historically been very effective at secretive political lobbying to protect its interests.

Late in summer 1990 members of the National Association of Life Underwriters (NALU) amassed for their annual conference, as they had done exactly one hundred times before. Despite the longevity of their association, this year's meeting was clouded over by universal concern about "the nation's growing health crisis" and what that implied for the future of life underwriters. Wasting no time engaging the looming crisis head on, the association decisively renamed a committee. The Health and Employee Benefits Committee was replaced with the Association of Health Insurance Agents (AHIA). Some participants expressed concern about this renaming because there already existed an embarrassingly similar organization, the National Association of Health Underwriters (NAHU). No problem, implied outgoing NALU president Robert J. Warnecke: More is better (Roxberry 1990).

Carl Schramm, president of the powerful Health Insurance Association of America (HIAA), understands clearly that change is in the air. His goal is to make sure that the health insurance industry does not suffer financially from that change. He advocates, for example, both private and public health insurance sectors, with the public sector picking up the health insurance tab for those who are unable to pay enough to the private sector. NALU executive vice-president Jack E. Bobo apparently agrees, adding the myopic insight that "innovative products . . . will deal effectively with these issues" (Roxberry 1990). The public-private split would be a dandy situation for the health insurance industry because it is in fact the same structure that benefits the enterprise currently. The commercial insurance industry keeps the profitable but nevertheless shrinking sector of the health insurance market and taxpayers subsidize the growing balance. Under this arrangement the insurers continue to support life-styles to which they have long been accustomed and the public sector foots the bill for the unprofitable sector of the market while relieving political pressure for meaningful, comprehensive health care reform.

Although leaders in the insurance industry do not seem to be involved in a vigorous public debate about their future course, they have many widely aired ideas regarding who is to blame for current problems. NALU president John N. Neighbors believes that the media are tired of the savings and loan scandal and are pestering the insurance industry to make up for slack news. NALU executive vice-president Bobo feels that the problem is the high cost of malpractice litigation (Roxberry 1990). Edward Blume, a lobbyist for the Wisconsin Association of Life and Health Insurers, blames state-mandated health insurance benefits such as those enforcing coverage for chiropractic services (Wis. Gubernatorial

Candidate Proposes 1990). Dr. Alain Enthoven, professor of management at Stanford University and sympathetic speaker at the 1990 annual meeting of the Health Insurance Association of America, blames tax laws, employers, employees, organized labor, and doctors, among others (Freedman 1991).

Insurers Do Not Want Public-Sector National Health Insurance

Despite its confusion on some levels, the Health Insurance Association of America (HIAA) is very clear about what it does not want to see in the future—publicly administered national health insurance. A study completed by HIAA in summer 1990 demonstrated the potential horrors for the American people of a health care system without the guiding involvement of a commercial health insurance industry (Pullen 1990c). "Canadian Health Care: The Implications of Public Health Insurance" found that a Canadian-style system established in the United States would result in the following catastrophes, among others:

- Government expenditures would increase by a quarter of a trillion dollars.
- The individual states (rather than the federal government) would bear most of the increased financial burden.
- Taxes would increase dramatically or the defense budget would have to be cut by 62 percent.
- Medical services and procedures would be rationed.

Fortunately for the health insurance industry its leaders have a weapon in their political and ideological arsenal other than renamed committees and self-serving studies. They have money. Four major corporate sellers of health insurance—American Family Corporation, the Travelers, Metropolitan, and Prudential—are all on the federal election commission's list of top fifty corporate campaign contributors. American Family Corporation is eighth on the list, outdistancing multinational corporations such as Ford Motor Co. and Boeing (The Crisis In Health Insurance 1990). According to a survey by the Center for Responsive Politics, in 1990 the insurance industry gave more money to congressional campaigns than any other branch of industry, contributing a total of $8.8 million for the 1990 elections. This was nearly $1 million more than the insurance industry gave for the previous 1988 elections, the biggest increase of all sectors of industry (Noonan and Pullen 1991). Toward the end of 1991 the Health Insurance Association of America admitted that it had recently committed $5 million to lobby fifteen key states to enact health insurance reforms forcing small businesses to provide health insurance to employees. The point of this high-pressure nationwide campaign is to head off federal reform of the health insurance industry (Health Insurers Campaign 1991).

Moreover, insurance industry public relations and "educational" departments lobby in their own unique and effective ways. In an interview with a Consumers Union reporter, the president of HIAA blurted out a most interesting admission:

> "We produce lots of research bulletins that are classy little numbers," HIAA president Schramm told CU. When the Pepper Commission issued its report last March, its recommendations for reforming sales practices in the small employer market were strikingly similar to those of the HIAA. "The Pepper Commission basically ceded the small-group issues to us," Schramm says. "They [the commission's recommendations] are our proposals." (The Crisis in Health Insurance 1990, 610)

Leaving no stone unturned by way of inundating the American public with self-serving insurance-thought, the 1991 annual meeting of HIAA featured speaker Michael Sheehan, "communications consultant." Some of his advice to an insurance industry under siege by legislators and the public included:

- "Counterprogram" by attacking the Canadian health care system.
- "Create a straw villain." This strategy is particularly effective if public prejudice already exists for the villain. It was suggested that an ideal bad guy might be government.
- "Divert attention" by finding someone else for the public to hate and then helping the public hate them. (Freedman 1991)

Conflict Between Agents and Carriers

There appears to be a growing conflict between independent agents, who actually deal face-to-face with irate victims of health insurance companies, and the insurers themselves. A recent letter written to the editor of the industry newspaper *National Underwriter* by Pat Farmer expresses this sentiment. Farmer was an independent life and health agent in Texas for several years and is currently marketing representative for a regional office:

> I chose to stop selling health insurance because of the many complaints I started receiving from people who at one time were "friends." Their complaint was first the 50 to 80 percent premium increase in a one year period, to the company taking six weeks to three months to respond to a claim. This was not with just one or two companies, but every company that I was contracted with. . . .

> I personally cannot see any answer besides a government controlled health plan. That is something I never thought that I would think or say. (Farmer 1991, 19)

In another recent letter to the same industry magazine, Florida independent agent Robert Taylor, president of Combined Insurance Services, Inc., made a similar point. After discussing how during the 1980s it became increasingly difficult to find insurance carriers willing to sell group health insurance to his prospects, Taylor observed:

> The major carriers have abandoned the small group market to go after the larger cash flows from larger groups. The market under fifty lives has been left to second tier carriers, who, for the most part, offer products with medical underwriting through associations and multi-employer Trusts. . . .
>
> The purported partnership between agents and carriers to provide coverage only works as long as the carriers want to play. When they take their ball and leave the game as they have in Florida, we all are losers and left to face the wrath of the uninsured public. (Taylor 1991, 17)

The Blues

A recent study by the Chicago-based national Blue Cross/Blue Shield Organization is quite interesting (Mulcahy 1990). It rigorously attacks commercial health insurers for engaging in shortsighted business activities that Blues management feels sure will bring new government regulations if not outright bypassing of the private insurance industry. The Blues criticize the commercials for withdrawing from markets such as individual and small-business health insurance, restricting business, and de-emphasizing certain health insurance products. Yet it is precisely through these methods that the commercials have taken a large chunk of market share away from the Blues in the past few decades. In any case, the Blues believe a national program based on the following points will reduce cost and access barriers:

- providing coverage to low- and moderate-income individuals and families through innovative programs;
- working with state governments and the National Association of Insurance Commissioners to achieve sensible insurance industry reforms such as waivers of state benefit mandates;
- promoting legislative reforms that encourage individuals to secure coverage, and improving government programs for the poor and disadvantaged;
- strengthening initiatives designed to promote effective and high-quality medical care;

- eliminating unnecessary duplication of medical services, fragmented delivery systems, and inefficient operations. (Mulcahy 1990, 54)

Commercial insurers should also be quite pleased with this program because it appears to fully protect their interests as well.

Insurance Lobbyists

Insurance lobbyists are at least as busy on the state level as on the federal level. There are more insurance lobbyists in nearly every state than any other type of lobbyist. In the early 1980s, for example, Massachusetts had about 400 registered lobbyists. Ford and General Motors each had one. Harvard and Common Cause each had two. Banks and labor unions had perhaps two or three dozen. The insurance industry alone fielded five dozen. Some insurance lobbyists have extraordinary access to state regulators. A 1979 GAO study found that approximately half of the state insurance commissioners came from the insurance industry and that about an equal number returned to it after their "public service" (Tobias 1982, 34–35, 270).

Model regulatory legislation drawn up by the National Association of Insurance Commissioners is often subsequently drafted into state legislation across the nation. There is, however, a slight flaw in the process. Insurance company personnel are typically the sole public representatives on the model legislation advisory committees (Tobias 1982, 270).

The situation is not substantially better in state legislatures. For example, "in North Carolina, in 1981, three of the eleven members of the Senate Insurance Committee owned and operated insurance agencies. A fourth was a director of Columbus Standard Life. In the House, four of seventeen committee members owned and operated insurance agencies; two more were lawyers representing insurance companies" (Tobias 1982, 170).

In 1987 Los Angeles County supervisor Kenneth Hahn asked the U.S. Justice Department to look into actions by the insurance industry "in a major conspiracy to obstruct the citizens' basic right to vote" (Reich 1987, 3). This scheme appeared to go beyond the normal activities of insurance lobbyists. Supervisor Hahn objected to the Association of California Insurance Companies and the California Trial Lawyers Association signing contracts to prevent the only two petition-circulating companies in California from agreeing to take on tort reform or insurance-related initiatives for any other groups. Supervisor Hahn himself had been interested at the time in promoting an initiative to implement progressive reform of auto insurance in the state.

In the same state a couple of years later, state senator Gary K. Hart (D-Santa Barbara) introduced legislation to prevent the insurance industry from giving campaign funds to candidates running for the new elective office of insurance commissioner. The replacement of a governor-appointed commissioner by a popularly elected insurance commissioner was part of the larger insurance consumer protection package in Proposition 103. The magnitude of the industry's financial resources is apparent from their struggle against Proposition 103 itself. The insurance industry dumped $65 million into that unsuccessful battle. Currently eleven states have elected insurance commissioners, but only a few of those states have enacted bans against insurance industry contributions to candidates (Ellis 1989).

Finally, if insurance lobbyists handing out tens of millions of dollars fail to deter meaningful insurance reform, insurers often sue or boycott. These responses have been seen most frequently to date in the area of auto insurance, where consumer groups and states have been particularly successful at winning insurance reform legislation. A recent example involves the state of New Jersey. Early in 1990 Gov. James Florio signed an automobile insurance reform act that the insurance industry did not like. Within a month Allstate Insurance Company had sued the governor, the state attorney general, and the former acting insurance commissioner. By that summer a number of the major auto insurers in New Jersey threatened to stop selling auto insurance in that state because they did not like the recently enacted automobile insurance reforms. Insurers threatening statewide boycott of auto insurance included ITT Hartford Group, CIGNA, Colonial Penn, and Crum & Forster. Gov. Jim Florio informed Hartford that if they ceased selling auto insurance in New Jersey they would not be allowed to sell any insurance at all in the state. The other insurers were warned that they might get the same treatment if they persisted (New Jersey Governor Threatens 1990; Dauer 1990). In California, eighty-four insurance companies sued the Department of Insurance in an attempt to kill new legislation that would roll back insurance rates and tighten up industry regulations. After bouncing all over the court system, the people of California finally won the case in mid-1991 (Insurer Group Loses 1991).

Summary

There is a great deal of activity at all levels of the polity to address the issues of cost and access to health care. The American people want access to health care, and the majority understand that it can be better accomplished without private health insurance. Organized labor increasingly understands this. Most congressional legislators, however, have responded to the insurance industry and to big business. Their proposals keep private health insurers intact and shift costs to employees. Exceptions to this pattern, however, include Representative Dellums's U.S. Health Service Act, Dr. Terris's A Progressive Proposal for a National Medical Care System, and the program advocated by Physicians for a National Health Program. State legislation is influenced by the same lobbies, and its effectiveness is further handicapped because the problem is national rather than local in scope and origin. Public health professionals and, increasingly, physicians and other providers understand the harmful role played by private health insurance.

chapter ten

Summary and Conclusions

The insurance industry in general and the health insurance industry in particular are currently undergoing massive structural changes. Some of the changes are the result of contradictions internal to the industry itself. Other changes are the result of contradictions between the insurance industry and forces outside it.

Perhaps the single greatest contradiction internally has been the drive by management to maximize profits on the one hand but remain nominally financially sound on the other. The drive for maximum profits has resulted in the accumulation of tens or hundreds of billions of dollars worth of high-risk but now almost worthless junk bonds and real estate. Profit seeking led to the excessive use of managing general agents (MGAs) to increase policy sales with the concurrent loss of corporate control over condition and total amount of sales. The quest for profits led to underfunded reserves, overreliance on unregulated reinsurers, and periodic massive underpricing of policies to get a bigger chunk of market share. All these financially risky profit-maximizing strategies were implemented in the context of deepening insurance business cycles, increasing loss of market share as a result of self-insurers and competing financial institutions, corporations frequently riddled with incompetent or corrupt management, and slipshod internal controls. The sum result of the convergence of these business strategies and the business environment has been a rapidly increasing number of insurance company insolvencies in recent years. Not only are there more insolvencies, but the insolvencies are reaching into the largest companies.

Hundreds of thousands of victims are created by the insolvencies. Some victims go bankrupt because of unpaid medical bills. Others are not able to find another health insurer who will sell them an affordable policy or any policy at all. Additional victims lose pensions that were to help pay medical costs. And most end up paying higher taxes or insurance premiums because of provisions in state guarantee funds.

The quest for maximum profits thrusts the insurance industry into severe contradictory relationships with regulators, the public, and other businesses. Ultimately, of course, the victims of insurance industry insolvencies frequently become bitter critics of the insurance industry. Periodic massive and unjustified premium price hikes likewise create a broad public political constituency advocating regulation if not outright elimination of the insurance industry. Fraudulent health insurers alienate small business on a regular basis, and unethical high-pressure agents regularly bilk the elderly and convert them into enemies of private insurance. Tens of millions of persons who were denied health insurance or were priced out of the insurance market have little appreciation for a system dominated by private health insurers. In this manner the insurance industry has manufactured its own intense political opposition, and it continues to do so with unrelenting zeal.

Consequences of the Elimination of Private Health Insurance

Contrary to a popular if typically unstated assumption, the insurance industry as a whole will not collapse with the elimination of private health insurance. As noted in Chapter 2, accident and health insurance premiums account for only 2.2 percent of all premiums in the property/casualty side of the industry and less than a quarter of all premiums on the life/health side of the industry. Furthermore, health insurance is decidedly less profitable than most other lines of insurance. It is often used merely as a loss leader in order to get a foot in the door to sell more profitable lines such as commercial liability or life. In fact during the past two or three years a number of major insurers have dropped personal and small-business lines of health insurance altogether. This accounts for some of the thousands of insurance employees that have been laid off in recent years.

Available figures indicate that 164,000 employees, about 12 percent of all private insurance industry employees, are primarily involved with health insurance (U.S. Department of Commerce 1990, 490). Recent layoffs in the industry may have already reduced this figure somewhat. In the event of elimination of private health insurance for publicly covered services, some of these employees would be retired early, others would be transferred, and perhaps some would find employment within the new national health system. In other comparable national health systems, there usually remains an active health insurance industry in the niches. For example, private health insurance might be available for an upgraded private hospital room or for international travel.

Nevertheless, most of these employees would probably be laid off, and the situation of unemployed workers is always a serious issue. Despite the fact that all 164,000 health insurance workers total less than 2 percent of all officially unemployed workers in the United States at the time of this writing, these individuals are working people who will have been caught in a historical restructuring of the industry quite outside their control. Perhaps a special provision in legislation establishing a national health system could provide for extended unemployment benefits, retraining, and outplacing for those displaced by the elimination of private health insurance. Clearly the general issue of economic transformation and unemployment is a national issue and can be managed effectively only in the context of comprehensive full-employment legislation. In any case, the guarantee of adequate access to health care for tens of millions of U.S. residents who now lack it (including unemployed persons) must remain the compelling social issue.

Emerging Social Forces Coalesce to Replace Private Health Insurance

The crucial factor is this: A few percent less than two-thirds of the American people prefer a system with no private health insurers (Blendon 1989). Apparently no comparable overwhelming majority of Congress can afford to share this popular wisdom. Virtually all current high-visibility proposed legislation assumes a probable or definite major role for the insurance industry. Conversely, proposed legislation such as Rep. Ron Dellums's (D-Calif.) U.S. Health Service Act, which specifically abolishes private health insurance, cannot get out of committee to become part of the national debate on health care reform. Popular will understands the social consequences of the private health industry, but congressional will is all too influenced by the insurance industry's vast resources.

It is in the interest of most physicians to support a national health system that eliminates the role of private health insurance. Many physicians understand this and struggle for the position through organizations such as Physicians Forum, Physicians for a National Health Program, and the American College of Physicians. The entire spectrum of public health professionals understands that private health insurance is antithetical to the basic principles of public health. They struggle for an alternative national health system through the American Public Health Association, the National Association for Public Health Policy, and other similar organizations. Progressive elements and entire unions within AFL-CIO understand that private health insurance is anathema to the health of working people. Several unions such as the Oil, Chemical, and Atomic Workers, United Auto Workers, and the American Federation of State, County, and Municipal Employees publicly support national health programs that feature the elimination of private health insurance. The struggle for this position still goes on at the highest levels of AFL-CIO. Industry leaders such as Lee Iacocca and Willis Goldbeck, past president of the Washington Business Group, have visibly warmed to national health insurance programs that may eliminate or reduce the role of private health insurers. Polls and trade organizations that represent small businesses indicate their receptivity also. The constituency to develop a national health system predicated on the elimination of private health insurance is inexorably building and will inevitably overcome.

bibliography

Advertising Claims Lead to Fines in Kansas. 1990. *Best's Insurance Management Reports, Life/Health.* January 22.

Aetna to Acquire All of Partners HMO. 1990. *Best's Insurance Management Reports, Life/Health.* January 22.

Aetna to Halt Individual Health Sales. 1990. *Best's Insurance Management Reports, Life/Health.* March 26.

A. M. Best Lowers Equitable Life's Rating. 1991. *Best's Insurance Management Reports, Life/Health.* June 17.

American Public Health Association. 1989a. *An Assessment of Selected National Health Program Proposals.* Draft. Washington, D.C.

______. 1989b. *A National Health Program for All of Us.* Pamphlet. Washington, D.C.

______. 1989c. *Sense of Congress Resolution.* April 24. Washington, D.C.

Angier, Natalie. 1990. Study Finds Uninsured Receive Less Hospital Care. *New York Times.* September 12.

Anglo-American Owes Louisiana $31 Million. 1990. *Best's Insurance Management Reports, Life/Health.* August 20.

Ansberry, Clare. 1988. Dumping the Poor. *Wall Street Journal.* November 29.

Appellate Court Revives Antitrust Suit. 1991. *Best's Insurance Management Reports, Life/Health.* June 24.

Arndt, Sheril. 1990a. Antitrust Exemption Under Fire in Many States. *National Underwriter, Life & Health.* September 3.

______. 1990b. Blues' HMO Plans Recorded Net Gain of $55M Last Year. *National Underwriter, Life & Health.* September 3.

Berg, Eric N. 1990. Rate Shift Called Peril for Insurers. *New York Times.* June 21, C6(N).

______. 1991a. Once-Paternal Insurers Trim Jobs. *New York Times.* April 18, C1(N), D1(L).

______. 1991b. Insurance Giants No Longer Ask People to Be All Things to All People; Many Are Abandoning Entire Areas Coverage. *New York Times.* February 7, A1(N), A1(L).

Berner, Mark, and J. Andrew Rahl, Jr. 1991. Defending Against the Tide of Junk Defaults. *National Underwriter, Life & Health.* May 6.

Bernstein, Aaron. 1990. Making It Pay to Stay Healthy. *Business Week.* May 21.

Best's Aggregates & Averages, Life-Health 1990. 1990. Oldwick, N. J.: A. M. Best Company.

Best's Aggregates & Averages, Property-Casualty 1990. 1990. Oldwick, N.J.: A. M. Best Company.

Bill Penalizing Insurers for Late Payments Sent to Louisiana Governor. 1990. *Best's Insurance Management Reports, Life/Health.* June 2.

Blendon, Robert J. 1989. Three Systems: A Comparative Survey. *Health Management Quarterly.* First Quarter.

Bodenheimer, Thomas. 1990. Should We Abolish the Private Health Insurance Industry? *International Journal of Health Sciences* 20:199–220.

Bradley, Barbara, and Robert P. Hey. 1988. Investigators Target Health Care Kickbacks. *Christian Science Monitor.* December 7.

Brostoff, Steven. 1990a. Agents/Companies Fight to Save McCarran Act. *National Underwriter, Life & Health.* July 2.

______. 1990b. Employer, Union Coalition Seeks Health Care Reform. *National Underwriter, Life & Health.* April 2.

______. 1991a. Democrats Unveil Health Proposal. *National Underwriter, Life & Health.* June 10.

______. 1991b. Sen. Says: Investigate Exec. Life. *National Underwriter, Life & Health.* May 20.

______. 1991c. Treasury Is Studying the Industry. *National Underwriter, Life & Health.* February 4.

Butler, Patricia A. 1988. *Too Poor to Be Sick.* Washington, D.C.: American Public Health Association.

Calif. Establishes Life/Health Guaranty Funds. 1991. *Best's Insurance Management Reports, Life/Health.* February 11.

California Still HMO Hotbed as Pru Moves in with HMO Plan. 1990. *National Underwriter, Life & Health.* September 10.

Calif. Takes Action Against Two Insurers. 1990. *Best's Insurance Management Reports, Life/Health.* August 13.

Canadians Like Their System. 1990. *Ammo.* United Auto Workers. September.

Caprino, Mariann. 1991. Most Insurers Financially Solid, New Ratings Show. *Anchorage Daily News [Associated Press].* November 7.

Caspar, Jennifer. 1990. Health Plans Go Back to Basics. *Washington Business.* July 16.

CBOT Sets Oct. 1 Launch for Insurance Futures. 1991. *Best's Insurance Management Reports, Life/Health.* March 4.

Census Heightens National Health Insurance Issue. 1991. *Nation's Health.* May/June.

Citizen Action Study Exposes Insurance Industry Inefficiency. 1990. *Washington Citizen Action News.* Fall.

Cleary Calls for Economic Reform. 1990. *Allegro.* October.

Colatosti, Camille. 1990. Coping with the Health Crisis. *Allegro.* October.

Committee Passes Bill to Limit McCarran-Ferguson. 1990. *Best's Insurance Management Reports, Life/Health.* June 25.

Companies Being Forced to Share Higher Health Costs. 1990. *Anchorage Times [Associated Press].* June 5.

Cost of Health Care Benefits Soars. 1990. *Health Security News.* February/March.

Council for Responsible Genetics. 1990. Position Paper on Genetic Discrimination. *New Solutions* (Summer):81–85.

Council on Medical Care, National Association for Public Health Policy. 1989. A Progressive Proposal for a National Medical Care System. *Journal of Public Health Policy* (Winter):533–538.

Cox, Brian. 1991. Insurance Receivers Form a Networking Society. *National Underwriter, Life & Health.* November 25.

Crenshaw, Albert B. 1991. Insurance: A Crisis of Confidence. *Washington Post.* July 21.

The Crisis in Health Insurance. 1990. *Consumer Reports.* Parts 1 & 2. August and September.

Crosson, Cynthia. 1990. UNUM, Hospital Team Up for At Home LTC. *National Underwriter, Life & Health.* August 6.

———. 1991a. Hefty Real Estate Losses Predicted. *National Underwriter, Life & Health.* May 6.

———. 1991b. Managed Care Sales Create New World at Cigna. *National Underwriter, Life & Health.* June 3.

Danielson, David A., and Arthur Mazer. 1986. The Massachusetts Referendum for a National Health Program. *Journal of Public Health Policy* (Summer):161–173.

Dauer, Christopher. 1990. Allstate Sues N.J. Governor Florio. *National Underwriter, Property & Casualty.* April 16.

D.C. City Council Approves Insurance Relief for Clinic. 1990. *Modern Healthcare.* October 15.

Details of Champion Investigation Released; Louisiana Gov. Signs High-Risk Health Care Bill. 1990. *Best's Insurance Management Reports, Life/Health.* July 9.

Eckholm, Erik. 1991. Health Benefits Found to Deter Job Switching. *New York Times.* September 26.

Ellis, Virginia. 1989. Ban Sought on Insurers' Contributions. *Los Angeles Times.* January 20.

Employer Insurance Costs Jump 20 Percent in 1989. 1990. *Anchorage Daily News.* January 30.

Employers Cut Back on Health Benefits. 1990. *Nation's Health.* July.

Equitable's Surplus Declines to $1.1 Billion. 1991. *Best's Insurance Management Reports, Life/Health.* March 11.

Ex-Wyoming Commissioner Sentenced. 1991. *Best's Insurance Management Reports, Life/Health.* March 4.

Farmer, Pat. 1991. Letter to the editor. *National Underwriter, Life & Health.* June 17.

Fenske, Doris. 1990. Regulatory Inconsistency on SAP Violations Not Good for Solvency, Belth Warns. *Best's Insurance Management Reports, Life/Health.* August 27.

Ferling, Rhona L. 1991. The LTC Market: Agents Learning the Ropes. *Best's Insurance Management Reports, Life/Health.* March 4.

Fewer HMOs Controlled by Hospitals—Report. 1990. *Modern Healthcare.* October 15.

Fisher, Mary Jane. 1989. ISO Cites "Constant Criticism." *National Underwriter, Property & Casualty.* May 1.

______. 1990. Ex-Agents in House Against McCarran Repeal. *National Underwriter, Life & Health.* August 20.

______. 1991. AIDS Group Stages Protest in Front of HIAA Offices. *National Underwriter, Life & Health.* May 20.

Fla. Commissioner Wants to Fingerprint Agents. 1990. *Best's Insurance Management Reports, Life/Health.* March 5.

Florida Insurance Consumer Advocate Named. 1990. *Best's Insurance Management Reports, Life/Health.* August 27.

Fogel, Richard L. 1991. *Insurance Regulation: Assessment of the National Association of Insurance Commissioners.* Statement before the Subcommittee on Oversight and Investigations, House Committee on Energy and Commerce. USGAO. May 22.

Former Wyoming Commissioner Indicted. 1990. *Best's Insurance Management Reports, Life/Health.* April 16.

Four Washington-Based Insurers Barred from Oregon. 1990. *Best's Insurance Management Reports, Life/Health.* February 12.

Fraser, Jill Andresky. 1990. The Travelers Rides into the Storm. *New York Times Magazine.* December 2.

Freedman, Marian. 1991. It's Time for Health Insurers to Show Their Stuff. *Best's Insurance Management Reports, Life/Health.* April 29.

Freudenheim, Milt. 1989a. Calling for a Bigger U.S. Health Role. *New York Times.* May 30.

______. 1989b. A Health-Care Taboo Is Broken. *New York Times.* May 8.

______. 1990a. Health Insurers' Changing Role. *New York Times.* January 16.

______. 1990b. Pressure Builds to Curb Medigap. *New York Times.* April 24.

______. 1990c. States Try to Cut Cost of Insurance for Medical Care; Policies May Cover Less; Industry Says Cheaper Plans Are Geared for 33 Million Who Lack Protection. *New York Times.* December 9.

Fuchs, Victor R., and James S. Hahn. 1990. How Does Canada Do It? *New England Journal of Medicine.* 323:884–890.

Gabel, Jon R., and Alan C. Monheit. 1983. Will Competition Plans Change Insurer-Provider Relationships? *Milbank Memorial Fund Quarterly* 61:614–640.

Gallup Poll Blasts Insurance Industry. 1990. *Best's Insurance Management Reports, Life/Health.* August 6.

Garamendi Outlines Health Insurance Reforms. 1991. *Best's Insurance Management Reports, Life/Health.* June 10.

Ginsburg, Jack A., and Deborah M. Prout. 1990. Access to Health Care. *Annals of Internal Medicine* 112:641–661.

Goodfriend, Herbert E. 1991. Prophets (sic) in Life Insurance. *Best's Insurance Management Reports, Life/Health.* April 29.

Gordon, Colin. 1991. Health Care the Corporate Way. *Nation.* March 25.

Governors Ask for Federal Action on Health Crisis. 1990. *Nation's Health.* May-June.

Great Republic Agrees to Settle Gay Discrimination Case. 1990. *Best's Insurance Management Reports, Life/Health.* May 14.

Great Republic Drops Health Plan. 1990. *Best's Insurance Management Reports, Life/Health.* June 4.

Group Calls for Nursing Home Insurance Probe. 1990. *Best's Insurance Management Reports, Life/Health.* March 5.

Haggerty, Alfred G. 1991. AIDS Org. Wins Jury Award Over Denial of Ins. *National Underwriter, Life & Health.* May 6.

Hartford Insurance Pays Record Fine to Connecticut. 1990. *Best's Insurance Management Reports, Life/Health.* April 23.

Havighurst, Clark C. 1988. The Questionable Cost-Containment Record of Commercial Health Insurers. In *Health Care in America,* edited by H. E. Frech III. San Francisco: Pacific Research Institute for Public Policy, 1988.

Hawaii Health Director Criticizes AIDS Insurance Plan. 1990. *Best's Insurance Management Reports, Life/Health.* May 7.

Health Care "Action Day" Set for Oct. 3. 1990. *AFL-CIO News.* August 7.

Health Care as a Basic Right. 1991. *Health Security News.* February-March.

The Health Care Crisis in America. 1985. Pamphlet by the Physicians Forum, Inc. Chicago, Ill.

Health Costs Take Health Bite out of Family Income. 1990. *Newsday.* May 1.

Health Insurance Association of America. n.d.(a). *Source Book of Health Insurance Data, 1981–2.* Washington, D.C.: Health Insurance Association of America.

———. n.d.(b). *Source Book of Health Insurance Data, 1989.* Washington, D.C.: Health Insurance Association of America.

Health Insurers Campaign to Stave Off Federal Reform. 1991. *Nation's Health.* November.

Health Security Action Council. 1988. Pamphlet by the Health Security Action Council. Washington, D.C.

The Health Security Partnership: An Equitable and Universal National Health Plan. n.d. Health Security Action Council Publication 8114.

Hey, Robert P., and Barbara Bradley. 1988. $450 Billion Industry Spawns Fraud, Abuse. *Christian Science Monitor.* December 7.

High Insurance Costs Cost American Jobs. 1990. *Ammo.* United Auto Workers. September.

Himmelstein, David U., and Steffie Woolhandler. 1986. Cost Without Benefit: Administrative Waste in U.S. Health Care. *New England Journal of Medicine* 314:441–445.

Himmelstein, David U., Steffie Woolhandler, and the Writing Committee of the Working Group on Program Design. 1989. A National Health Program for the United States: A Physicians' Proposal. *New England Journal of Medicine* 320:102–108.

House Subcommittee Passes Bill Limiting McCarran-Ferguson Act. 1990. *Best's Insurance Management Reports, Life/Health.* June 18.

Howard, Lisa. 1990. Ex-Wyoming Reg. Charged with Bribery. *National Underwriter, Property & Casualty.* April 23.

Indiana Bills Would Increase Commissioner's Power. 1990. *Best's Insurance Management Reports, Life/Health.* January 22.

Insurance Break Foreseen for the Fit. 1990. *New York Newsday.* October 6.

Insurance Canadian-Style: States Start to Explore Option. 1991. *Nation's Health.* July.

Insurance Services Office, Inc. 1987. *Insurance Services Office in a Competitive Marketplace: ISO's Role Within the Property/Casualty Industry.* ISO Insurance Issues Series. June.

Insurance Stock Trends. 1990. *Best's Insurance Management Reports, Life/Health.* January 15.

Insurer Group Loses Prop 103 Appeal. 1991. *Best's Insurance Management Reports, Life/Health.* June 10.

Insurers Paid $1 Billion in Aids-Related Claims in 1987. 1990. *Modern Healthcare.* November 5.

Insurers' Ratings May Slip. 1991. *Anchorage Daily News [Chicago Tribune].* October 2.

Intelligent Investing in Health Care. 1991. *Health Security News.* April-May.

Intindola, Brendan. 1991. AIDS Reserves Deemed Adequate. *National Underwriter, Life & Health.* April 22.

Jones, David C. 1990. Employers "Dumping" Health Risks in Ill. *National Underwriter, Property & Casualty.* April 9.

Justice Dept. Backs States in Antitrust Suit. 1990. *Best's Insurance Management Reports, Life/Health.* May 21.

Justice Department Indicts Louisiana Commissioner. 1990. *Best's Insurance Management Reports, Life/Health.* June 11.

Kenkel, Paul. 1990a. Faced with Inaction in Washington, States Forge Ahead with Plans to Cover Uninsured. *Modern Healthcare.* August 6.

______. 1990b. General Motors Drops Six HMOs, Brakes Enrollment in 19 Others in Effort to Cut Costs. *Modern Healthcare.* November 19.

______. 1990c. High Costs, Risks Cited in Blues Plan's Demise. *Modern Healthcare.* October 29.

______. 1990d. '91 Medicare Rates Have HMOs Eyeing Changes. *Modern Healthcare.* October 22.

______. 1990e. Who'll Pay Blues Plan's Bills? *Modern Healthcare.* October 22.

Kirkland, Lane. 1991. Remarks of AFL-CIO President Lane Kirkland to the American Medical Association National Leadership Conference. Press release, AFL-CIO Department of Information. February 17.

Kluepfel, Gail. 1990. A Lot of Talk But Still No National Health Plan. *Best's Insurance Management Reports, Life/Health.* July 2.

Knowles, Robert G. 1990. Southern States Hit Hard by Insolvencies. *National Underwriter, Property & Casualty.* April 9.

______. 1991a. Former Chief Examiner of North Carolina Is Indicted. *National Underwriter, Life & Health.* June 3.

______. 1991b. Ga. Regulator Hits Fraud with "Sting" Operations. *National Underwriter, Life & Health.* June 17.

Koco, Linda. 1990. Small Group Health Premium. *National Underwriter, Life & Health.* July 30.

______. 1991. HMOs Start Offering Point-of-Service Options. *National Underwriter, Life & Health.* February 11.

Kristof, Kathy M. 1991. Executive Life Seizure Stirs Fears of Crisis in Industry. *Los Angeles Times.* April 13.

Labor Research Association. 1989. Is Iaccoca for Real? Labor Should Not Depend on It. *Economic Notes.* July-August.

______. 1991. Health Care Debate. *Trade Union Advisor.* February 12.

Labaton, Stephen. 1988. Antitrust Actions Against Insurers. *New York Times.* April 4.

La. Bill Would Impose Special Damages on Insurers. 1990. *Best's Insurance Management Reports, Life/Health.* May 29.

La. Commissioner Gets 25 Years for Insurance Scheme. 1991. *Best's Insurance Management Reports, Life/Health.* June 17.

Laing, Jonathan R. 1990. Flawed Policies: Big Junk and Real-Estate Holdings Put Life Insurers at Risk. *Barrons.* October 1.

Lansner, Jonathan. 1991. *Anchorage Daily News [Orange County Register].* October 29.

Laudicina, Susan. 1988. State Health Risk Pools: Insuring the "Uninsurable." *Health Affairs* (Fall):97–108.

Law, Sylvia A. 1976. *Blue Cross: What Went Wrong?* 2nd. ed. New Haven: Yale University Press.

Lear, Walter. 1989. 46 to 18 Years Ago—The Physicians Forum for a National Health Program. *Physicians Forum Bulletin.* Fall.

Legislation to Regulate Medigap Industry Proposed. 1990. *Best's Insurance Management Reports, Life/Health.* May 29.

L/H Industry New Operating Results: Statutory Earnings Soar. 1990. *Best's Insurance Management Reports, Life/Health.* May 29.

Life/Health Corporate Changes—1989. 1990. *Best's Insurance Management Reports.* February 12.

Lipsen, Linda. 1990. Insurance Firms: Privileged Class. *New York Times.* June 5.

Louisiana Commissioner Granted Stay. 1990. *Best's Insurance Management Reports, Life/Health.* April 16.

McClure, Laura. 1990. Does a Reformed System Mean a Better System? *Allegro.* October. Reprinted from *Labor Notes,* July 1990.

McDonald, Gregory J. 1991. *Retiree Health: Company-Sponsored Plans Facing Increased Costs and Liabilities.* Testimony Before the Subcommittee on Health, Committee on Ways and Means, House of Representatives. Gaithersburg, Md.: GAO. May 6.

McGhee, Neil. 1991. 2nd Largest HMO in Mass. Faces Provider Revolt. *National Underwriter, Life & Health.* March 18.

Malis, Ira. 1990. Long-Term Care: A Growth Sector in the Insurance Business. *Best's Insurance Management Reports, Life/Health.* August 6.

Mandatory Insurance Is Backed by A.M.A. 1989. *New York Times.* June 22.

Marcus, Amy D., and Alecia Swasy. 1990. Cap on AIDS Benefit Wins Legal Round. *Wall Street Journal.* August 1.

Maryland Attorney General Warns of Illegal HMO Billing. 1990. *Modern Healthcare.* November 19.

Maxey, Brigitte. 1991. 26 Insurers Reporting Junk-Filled Portfolios. *Anchorage Daily News [Journal of Commerce].* May 10.

Md. Blue Cross/Blue Shield Loses Bid to Mutualize. 1991. *Best's Insurance Management Reports, Property/Casualty.* January 7.

Meakin, Thomas K. 1991. Our Rally Stretches into Its Fifth Month. *National Underwriter, Life & Health.* April 15.

Medical Plan Costs Expected to Skyrocket. 1991. *Best's Insurance Management Reports, Life/Health.* June 17.

Medigap Insurance: Better Consumer Protection Should Result from 1990 Changes to Baucus Amendment. 1991. Report to congressional requesters. Gaithersburg, Md.: GAO. March.

Medigap Insurance Reform. 1990. *Nation's Health.* December.

Mesche, Deborah. 1991. Feds, Insurers Vow to Cut Costs, Streamline Claims. *Anchorage Daily News [Associated Press].* November 6.

Michaels, Glenna. 1990. Universal Health Care: An Idea Whose Time Has Come. *Public Employee Press.* October 12.

Midwest Life Agrees to Supervision in Tex.; Parent Under Criminal Investigation in La. 1991. *Best's Insurance Management Reports, Life/Health.* March 25.

Millus, Albert. 1988. Analyzing the Case of the Attorney's General Antitrust Suits. *Risk Management.* October.

Missouri Blues Buys Pension Associates. 1990. *Modern Healthcare.* August 27.

More HMOs Posted Profits in '89; Premium Hikes Cited. 1990. *Modern Healthcare.* October 15.

Mulcahy, Colleen. 1990. Health Insurer "Tactics" Threaten Future: Blues. *National Underwriter, Life & Health.* September 3.

______. 1991a. Managed Care Assumptions "Untested, Unproven." *National Underwriter, Life & Health.* May 6.

______. 1991b. 300% Rise in "90 For Blues" HMOs. *National Underwriter, Life & Health.* June 10.

Nadel, Mark V. 1991. *Private Health Insurance: Problems Caused by a Segmented Market.* Gaithersburg, Md.: GAO. July.

National Center for Health Services Research. 1989. *Health Insurance Coverage in the U.S.* Washington, D.C.: USGPO.

National Health Care Campaign. 1987. State Campaigns Win Health Care Reform. *Health Care News.* July.

National Health Care Reform. 1991. Statement by the AFL-CIO Executive Council. Washington, D.C. February 19.

National Health Resolution Gaining Sponsors in Congress. 1990. *Nation's Health.* August.

Nazario, Sonia L. 1988. Life and Death: High Infant Mortality Is a Persistent Blotch on Health Care in U.S. *Wall Street Journal.* October 19.

Nevada Commissioner Resigns. 1991. *Best's Insurance Management Reports, Life/Health.* February 15.

Nev. Commissioner Put on Leave During Probe. 1991. *Best's Insurance Management Reports, Life/Health.* February 11.

New Head of National Governors' Assn. Advocates National Healthcare System. 1990. *Modern Healthcare.* August 13.

New Jersey Governor Threatens Hartford Group. 1990. *Best's Insurance Management Reports, Life/Health.* August 20.

New Jersey Insurance Official Charged with Taking Bribes. 1990. *New York Times.* July 8.

New Study Blasts Insurance Paperwork Costs. 1990. *Washington Citizen Action News.* Summer.

New York Department of Health. 1990. UNY*Care—A Proposal: Revision I. New York. May 10.

1989 Life/Health Year-End Financial Results. 1990. *Best's Insurance Management Reports, Life/Health.* April 16.

N.J. Appeals Court Upholds Insurance Law; Five Years Required to Withdraw from Market. 1991. *Best's Insurance Management Reports, Life/Health.* June 17.

Noonan, Brendan, and Rick Pullen. 1991. Insurance PACS Throw Weight and Money Around. Best's Insurance Management Reports, Life/Health. June 3.

Nursing Introduces Its National Health Strategy to the Public. 1991. *Public Policy Bulletin.* March.

N.Y. Court Permits AIDS Testing. 1990. *Best's Insurance Management Reports, Property/Casualty.* December 24.

N.Y. Court Says State Must Restore Guaranty Fund. 1991. *Best's Insurance Management Reports, Life/Health.* April 8.

100 Largest Life/Health Writers Dominate Premium Growth. 1991. *Best's Insurance Management Reports, Life/Health.* May 28.

Pa. Regulator Upheld on Small Groups. 1991. *National Underwriter, Life & Health.* April 1.

Philadelphia Blues to Pay $2 Million to Settle Charges. 1990. *Modern Healthcare.* October 8.

Phillips, Pat. 1990. ACP Stands Alone on Total Access. *Medical World News.* May 28.

Physicians Who Profit from Tests Order More of Them, Study Claims. 1990. *Anchorage Daily News [Associated Press].* April 12.

Pickett, George. 1976. President's Column. *Nation's Health.* December.

Piller, Dan. AIDS Claims Crush Hasn't Hit. 1991. *Anchorage Daily News [Fort Worth Star-Telegram].* November 9.

Pound, Edward, and Walt Bogdanich. 1989. Medical Mess: Has Medicare Paid Out Billions Actually Owed by Private Insurers? *Wall Street Journal.* April 7.

Primeau, Marty. 1990. Risky Business. *Spirit.* July.

Pullen, Rick. 1990a. Assault on McCarran-Ferguson Continues in Senate. *Best's Insurance Management Reports, Life/Health.* July 2.

______. 1990b. Bill Earmarks Federal Funds to Stop Medigap Abuses. *Best's Insurance Management Reports, Life/Health.* March 26.

______. 1990c. HIAA Study Critical of Canadian Health Care System. *Best's Insurance Management Reports, Life/Health.* July 2.

______. 1990d. Long-Term Care Policies on Increase. *Best's Insurance Management Reports, Life/Health.* July 2.

______. 1990e. P/C Insolvencies Could Rival S&L Debacle; Healthy Insurers Urged to Prevent Disaster. *Best's Insurance Management Reports, Life/Health.* June 18.

———. 1990f. Senate Hears Testimony on MEWA Fraud. *Best's Insurance Management Reports, Life/Health.* May 29.

———. 1991a. GAO Finds Medigap Abuses Continue. *Best's Insurance Management Reports, Life/Health.* June 24.

———. 1991b. HHS, AFL-CIO Disagree over National Health Care. *Best's Insurance Management Reports, Life/Health.* February 25.

———. 1991c. Justice Dept. to Investigate Insurance Industry for Fraud. *Best's Insurance Management Reports, Life/Health.* April 8.

———. 1991d. NAIC Urges Federal Criminal Code for Insurance Fraud. *Best's Insurance Management Reports, Life/Health.* April 29.

Randall, Robert F. 1990. 88% of Firms Curb Health Benefit Costs. *Management Accounting.* April.

Reich, Kenneth. 1987. Hahn Seeks U.S. Probe of Legal Insurance Lobbies. *Los Angeles Times.* November 13.

Report Cites Racial Discrepancies in Medical Care. 1990. *New York Times.* May 2.

Riskin, Benjamin. 1991. Letter to author. September 21.

Robinson, Sherry. 1990. MEWAs: Small Firms Often Victimized. *Albuquerque Journal.* July 9.

Roxberry, Megan. 1990. Life Producers Grapple with Health Care Crisis. *Best's Insurance Management Reports, Life/Health.* September 17.

Rubin, Harvey W. 1987. *Dictionary of Insurance Terms.* New York: Barron's Educational Series.

Ruling Exempts Self-Funded Plans from Some State Laws. 1990. *Modern Healthcare.* December 3.

Russo, Marty. 1991. Our Health System Sorely Needs Repairs. *New York Newsday.* June 3.

Short, P., A. Monheit, and K. Beauregard. 1989. *A Profile of Uninsured Americans.* National Medical Expenditure Survey Research Findings 1, National Center for Health Services Research and Health Care Technology Assessment. Rockville, Md.: Public Health Service.

Some Insurers Concede McCarran-Ferguson Changes. 1991. *Best's Insurance Management Reports, Life/Health.* May 6.

Starr, Paul. 1982. *The Social Transformation of American Medicine.* New York: Basic Books.

The State of California v. Hartford Fire Insurance Company, et al. 1988. Submitted to U.S. District Court for the Northern District of California. March 22.

The State of Texas vs. Insurance Services Office, Inc., et al. 1988. Submitted by the Texas Attorney General's Office in the District Court of Travis County, Texas.

Study Hits HMOs' Contracts, Medicaid Enrollee Care Limits. 1990. *Modern Healthcare.* September 3.

Support for National Health Care Grows. 1989. *Benefits Today.* Bureau of National Affairs. December 29.

Taylor, Robert E. 1991. Letter to the editor. *National Underwriter, Life & Health.* May 13.

Texas Fraud Investigation Results in Indictments. 1990. *Best's Insurance Management Reports, Life/Health.* June 2.

Texas Orders Health Insurer to Cease Business. 1990. *Best's Insurance Management Reports, Life/Health.* July 23.

Thompson, Terri. 1990. Checking Up on Life Insurers. *U.S. News and World Report.* May 28.

Tobias, Andrew. 1982. *The Invisible Bankers.* New York: Linden Press/Simon & Schuster.

Tolchin, Martin. 1988. Welfare Denied to Many of Poor Over Paperwork. *New York Times.* October 29.

Townsend, Frederick S. 1991. High Risk Assets: 140% of 1990 Total Surplus. *National Underwriter, Life & Health.* June 3.

Transport Life May Lose N.J. License. 1990. *Best's Insurance Management Reports, Life/Health.* September 17.

Uchitelle, Louis. 1990. Seeking U.S. Aid for Health Care. *New York Times.* May 21.

Unions Yes—But. 1990. *Nation.* September 17.

Universal Health Care Bill Introduced. 1991. *Best's Insurance Management Reports, Life/Health.* June 3.

U.S. Congress. 1986. House. Select Committee on Aging. Subcommittee on Health and Long-Term Care. *Catastrophic Health Insurance: The "Medigap" Crisis.* Report by the chair. 99th Cong., 2nd sess.

______. 1988a. House. Committee on Energy and Commerce. Hearing Before the Subcommittee on Commerce, Consumer Protection, and Competitiveness. *Developments in State Insurance Regulation.* 100th Cong., 1st. sess.

______. 1988b. House. Committee on Energy and Commerce. Hearing Before the Subcommittee on Commerce, Consumer Protection, and Competitiveness. *Private Health Insurance for the Elderly.* 100th Cong., 1st sess.

______. 1988c. House. Committee on Energy and Commerce. Hearing Before the Subcommittee on Commerce, Consumer Protection, and Competitiveness. *State Lawsuits Against Insurance Companies.* 100th Cong., 2nd sess.

______. 1988d. House. Select Committee on Aging. Joint Hearing Before the Subcommittee on Health and Long-Term Care and the Subcommittee on Housing and Consumer Interests. *Nursing Home Insurance: Exploiting Fear for Profit?* 100th Cong., 1st sess.

______. 1988e. Office of Technology Assessment. *Healthy Children: Investing in the Future.* Washington, D.C.: USGPO.

______. 1988f. Office of Technology Assessment. *Medical Testing and Health Insurance.* Washington, D.C.: USGPO.

______. 1989a. House. Committee on Energy and Commerce. Hearing Before the Subcommittee on Oversight and Investigations. *Insurance Company Failures.* 101st Cong., 1st sess.

______. 1989b. House. Committee on Ways and Means. Hearing Before the Subcommittee on Health. *Fiscal Year 1990 Budget Issues Relating to Physician Incentive Payments by Prepaid Health Plans.* 101st Cong., 1st sess.

———. 1989c. House. Committee on Ways and Means. Hearing Before the Subcommittee on Health. *Health Insurance and the Uninsured.* 101st Cong., 1st sess.

———. 1989d. House. H.R. 2500. *U.S. Health Service Act.* Introduced by Rep. Dellums (D-Calif.). 101st Cong., 1st sess.

———. 1989e. Joint Economic Committee. Subcommittee on Education and Health. *Medical Alert.* Staff report summarizing the hearings "The Future of Health Care in America." 101st Cong., 1st. sess.

———. 1989f. Senate. *Basic Health Benefits for All Americans Act.* Report together with minority views to accompany S. 768.

———. 1990a. House. Committee on Energy and Commerce. Report by the Subcommittee on Oversight and Investigations. *Failed Promises: Insurance Company Insolvencies.* 101st Cong., 2nd sess.

———. 1990b. House. Committee on Ways and Means. Hearing Before the Subcommittee on Oversight. *Employer-Sponsored Retiree Health Insurance.* 101st Cong., 1st sess.

———. 1990c. House. Select Committee on Aging. *Building an American Health System: Journey Toward a Healthy and Caring America.* Report by the chair. 101st Cong., 2nd sess.

U.S. Department of Commerce. 1975. *Historical Statistics of the United States, Colonial Times to 1970.* Washington, D.C.: Bureau of Census.

———. 1990. Bureau of Census. *Statistical Abstract of the United States, 1990.* Washington, D.C.: USGPO.

U.S. General Accounting Office. 1990. *Health Insurance Cost Increases Lead to Coverage Limitations and Cost Shifting.* Report to congressional requesters. Gaithersburg, Md. May.

———. 1991a. *Canadian Health Insurance: Lessons for the United States.* Report to the chairman, Committee on Government Operations, House of Representatives. Gaithersburg, Md. June.

———. 1991b. Medicaid: *HCFA Needs Authority to Enforce Third-Party Requirements on States.* Report to the chairman, Committee on Government Operations, House of Representatives. Gaithersburg, Md. April.

Wagner, Lynn. 1990a. Framework for Reform. *Modern Healthcare.* September 3.

———. 1990b. Study Critical of Insurers' Overhead Costs. *Modern Healthcare.* October 15.

Welles, Chris, and Christopher Farrell. 1989. Insurance: An Industry Under Siege. *Business Week.* August 21.

Wis. Gubernatorial Candidate Proposes Increased Regulation of Health Insurers. 1990. *Best's Insurance Management Reports, Life/Health.* May 14.

Woolhandler, Steffie, and David U. Himmelstein. 1989. Resolving the Cost/Access Conflict: The Case for a National Health Program. *Journal of General Internal Medicine* 4:54–60.

———. 1991. The Deteriorating Administrative Efficiency of the U.S. Health Care System. *New England Journal of Medicine.* May 2.

Zinman, David. 1990. The National Insurance Campaign. *Newsday.* June 5.

about the book and author

The private health insurance industry is unable to provide nearly 40 million Americans with basic health care. Relying on data from a wide range of publications about this secretive industry, Lawrence D. Weiss investigates the causes of the industry's problems and analyzes the social effects of the growing crisis. The causes include excessive overhead costs, widespread inefficiency, and exemptions from antimonopoly regulations; the social effects include small businesses' inabilities to provide adequate coverage for their employees, the reluctance of many carriers to insure certain social groups, and the disproportionate burden on minorities. Addressing these dilemmas, Lawrence D. Weiss offers a timely and important analysis of the health insurance crisis in America.

Lawrence D. Weiss is medical sociologist at the University of Alaska at Anchorage. He earned his doctoral degree in Sociology at SUNY–Binghamton and completed a post-doctoral degree at Harvard School of Public Health. He is author of numerous articles on national and international health issues.

index